Britannia Unchained

Britannia Unchained

Global Lessons for Growth and Prosperity

Kwasi Kwarteng *MP for Spelthorne*

Priti Patel *MP for Witham*

Dominic Raab *MP for Esher and Walton*

Chris Skidmore *MP for Kingswood*

Elizabeth Truss *MP for South West Norfolk*

First published 2012 by
PALGRAVE MACMILLAN

Palgrave Macmillan in the UK is an imprint of Macmillan Publishers Limited, registered in England, company number 785998, of Houndmills, Basingstoke, Hampshire RG21 6XS.

Palgrave Macmillan in the US is a division of St Martin's Press LLC, 175 Fifth Avenue, New York, NY 10010.

Palgrave Macmillan is the global academic imprint of the above companies and has companies and representatives throughout the world.

Palgrave® and Macmillan® are registered trademarks in the United States, the United Kingdom, Europe and other countries

ISBN 978-1-137-03223-2   ISBN 978-1-137-03224-9 (eBook)
DOI 10.1057/9781137032249

A catalogue record for this book is available from the British Library.

A catalog record for this book is available from the Library of Congress.

10 9 8 7 6 5 4 3 2 1
21 20 19 18 17 16 15 14 13 12

Transferred to Digital Printing in 2013

Contents

Acknowledgements

The authors would like to thank for their assistance with research, advice and preparation of drafts Simon Clarke, Jonathan Dupont, James Earle, Sarah Fitch and Andrew Goodfellow.

We would especially like to thank Amber Stone-Galilee, our Commissioning Editor, whose enthusiasm has sustained the project from its inception to publication.

Finally, we would like to thank all those who have given permission for their material to be used in this work, including the BBC, the RSA, the Conference Board, Lex Deak and Bernard Bar-Natan.

Introduction

On 8 August 2011, 20-year-old Ashraf Rossli set out to cycle to a scared female friend. It was the middle of the London riots. A group of thugs got in his way. Ashraf tried to get past. He received a punch straight to the face, which broke his jaw in two places.[1] His attacker was 17-year-old Beau Isagba. At the age of 14, Beau had earned his first conviction for possession of a knife. At 16, he earned a second for possession of cannabis.[2]

Beau pulled Ashraf off his bike, and to the delight of his gang mates, threw him to the ground. Beau cycled away with his new bicycle. Ashraf sat dazed on the ground.

A few minutes later two young men approached. They asked if he was okay, and helped Ashraf to his feet. While Ashraf was still dazed, these young men took their opportunity to steal his PlayStation.

Their actions were recorded on another girl's mobile, and then placed up on YouTube for the world to see. So far, 6 million people have watched what was to become one of the iconic scenes of the London riots. Just a year before 2012's Jubilee and Olympic year, the world saw Britain at its worst.

Ashraf, an accountancy student from Malaysia, had been in Britain just one month. He was a hard working, ambitious student, who had scored a string of As in his exams at school.[3] He forgave his attackers. He told reporters that he was not angry,[4] that he still believed in Britain and that he was determined to stay.[5]

This episode symbolises some of the issues we wish to tackle in this book. Ashraf represents the best of a new ambitious, hard working, developing world. Sadly, Beau Isagba represents the worst of what some elements of Britain have become.

Britannia Unchained is a book about what Britain can learn from the rest of the world. As the world becomes more competitive, Britain will have to work harder to keep up. Britain has much to be optimistic about. The horror of the riots was an aberration, not an accurate picture of the day to day of London life. Nevertheless, if we are to prosper in future, we have to much learn from the Ashrafs of the world.

1

The latest economic crisis is only the most recent manifestation of more fundamental problems. In Britain, there has been too great a tendency to attribute results to fortune or background, coupled with a general reluctance to take hard decisions on economic policy. Britain has also suffered from a diminished work ethic and a culture of excuses.

In twenty-first-century Britain, more people look to others to solve their problems. The dependency culture has grown dramatically. By February 2012, 5.7 million people of working age in Britain were collecting some kind of benefits. At over 13 per cent of the working population, this is one of the highest proportions in the OECD.

It is now clear that, unless we get a grip of these problems, the next British generation will end up with a diminished share of the world's wealth and resources. It is also likely that the new ideas which will shape the world may come from India or Brazil, rather than Britain. The current crisis should be seen as a wake-up call to all Britons. There is no inevitability about the future. We need only look at Greece and Italy, or Germany and Canada, to see the different paths taken by nations. Some decide to take control of their own destiny, while others manifestly fail to do so.

All five authors grew up in a period where Britain was improving its performance relative to the rest of the world. The 1980s, contrary to the beliefs of many on the left, were a successful decade for Britain. They were a time when, after the industrial chaos of the 1970s, business and enterprise began to flourish once more.

We want to see this spirit of innovation renewed. We know that Britain can be successful. The seeds of this revival are there. We also see pockets of inspiration around the country that, if unleashed, could propel us into the superleague rather than the also-rans. Our research capability is the best in the world. We have technological companies who work tirelessly on new products. There are many stories of people who have earned enormous success through their own efforts.

But changing Britain's fortunes needs a relentless energy and determined focus. Vitally we will need to be tougher in taking on vested interests. These occur in lots of guises, through bureaucratic inertia, and many of the perks which a generous welfare state lavished on previous generations. We have to ensure that the general climate for business is attractive. This means that we should stop indulging in irrelevant debates about sharing the pie between manufacturing and services, the north and the south, women and men. Instead, we should focus on trying to make it easier for firms to recruit people and ensuring the tax burden is less onerous.

To achieve these goals we think it is helpful to take a step back and go on a worldwide journey, so to speak. In the long run, what goes on in Sao Paulo, Beijing and Mumbai may well affect the future of Western Europe more than partisan disputes about precisely how fast to cut public spending.

The recent crisis in the Eurozone has been the story of European countries' failure to adapt to international competition. Countries like Greece and Italy, which adopted the euro, found that their costs became too high and effectively priced them out of international markets. Both countries saw a marked decline in productivity. This development affected these countries as much as particular decisions their governments made relating to public spending.

The situation of Greece, Spain and Italy in 2012 should be a warning to Britons about some of the dangers ahead. The really deep austerity cuts facing Greece and Italy have been avoided, so far, in Britain. Yet many of the structural problems in the economies of the countries of Southern Europe are shared by Britain: a large, bloated public sector; increasingly large liabilities regarding pensions in the public sector; too much spending and too little growth; poor productivity.

Britain's continued use of its own currency, the pound sterling, has shielded it from the worst effects of the fiscal crisis affecting Europe. But the problems Britain faces are, like those of European countries, long-standing. Britain's own cultural history, where issues of class are particularly potent, has also made the situation more critical. Beyond the statistics and economic theories, there remains a sense in which many of Britain's problems lie in the sphere of cultural values and mindset. These are, naturally, more difficult to analyse than economic problems. They are also harder for politicians and commentators to address.

After the financial crisis of 2008, many people in the West began to question the basis of free market capitalism. 'Business' became a dirty word. The 'fat cat' bankers, who had all grown extremely rich, were castigated on all sides of the political divide. Yet, in the emerging economies of Asia, South America and Africa, economic progress continued unabated. In these countries individual initiative and free enterprise continued to drive progress. Millions of people are being pulled out of poverty across the world by the simple processes of capitalism. *Britannia Unchained* is unembarrassed about its support for business, the profit motive and the individual drive of the wealth creator.

The term 'globalisation' is a cliché. However, it is certain that, for the first time in centuries, the world economy is being driven by what happens outside Europe and North America. At the same time, many parts of the old world are fighting back. Germany has embarked on a programme of welfare reform. Countries in Scandinavia are pursuing labour market reform. Canada has successfully cut its deficit. It makes sense then for anybody involved in politics in Britain to engage fully with what's going on in the wider world. *Britannia Unchained* is an attempt to do just that.

Each chapter of the book looks at a particular aspect of economy and society in a particular country, or countries, and tries to draw general conclusions about the lessons that can be learned.

The first chapter, 'The Chains', sets out the central question of the book. It asks whether we are inevitably destined for national decline. Britain has often wallowed in self-pity as the glories of Empire have ebbed away. The chapter argues that Britain is once again facing the same loss of confidence last seen in the 1970s.

Chapter 2, 'A Tale of Two Nations', looks at the Canadian approach to public spending. It has been striking how effective Canada has been in meeting the challenges of the financial crisis. It is widely known that the position of Canadian banks has been much stronger than their counterparts in the United States and Europe. Chapter 2 also looks at how Canada reformed its government in the 1990s. After a decade of reckless spending Canada successfully managed to cut its spending and start upon the way to growth and more sustainable development.

Chapter 3 is about educational aspiration in Britain. This chapter, entitled 'Revenge of the Geeks', shows how education is viewed in India and other thriving new economies and contrasts these with Britain, where the ideals of celebrity culture and instant fame are prevalent. In many opinion surveys conducted in Britain it has been found that young people aspire to be fashion models or professional footballers ahead of becoming lawyers, doctors or even scientists. We argue that one advantage of the rising economies is the emphasis they place on education. Young people in India and South Korea are more likely to work hard at school in order to enter well paid and respected professions. It is clear that a society motivated in this way will become, over a short period of time, more successful and productive. Chapter 2 gives suggestions as to what Britain can learn in this respect.

In Chapter 4, entitled 'Work Ethic', we explore the nature of the work ethic in South Korea, Singapore and Hong Kong and contrast this to that found in Britain. We ask ourselves, 'What is it about these countries that makes them so dynamic?' In this chapter we look at the way in which the state has made Britons idle. Our culture of instant gratification ignores the years of persistence that lie behind real success. Too many people in Britain, we argue, prefer a lie-in to hard work.

Chapter 5, entitled 'Buccaneers', is a wider exploration of the nature of business innovation and entrepreneurial drive. In this chapter the achievements of Israel, perhaps surprisingly to some, are celebrated in the area of science and technology. Israel has shown how venture capital can be attracted into exciting areas. This capital is particularly supportive of technological innovation and businesses which rely on what is sometimes called 'the knowledge economy'. Through the application of science and business acumen, exciting commercial opportunities often arise. Overshadowed by political concerns, Israel remains an underappreciated hub of scientific innovation. By contrast, it is a commonly observed feature of modern Britain that the state and bureaucracy have become more entrenched over the last decade. There is a feeling that initiative and individual enterprise have been stifled by an obsession with rules, regulations and 'health and safety'. This climate of excessive bureaucratic control has made Britain less competitive on the international scene.

The final chapter, 'Britannia Unchained', returns to the question of whether Britain is an old country, fated to gradual decline. It argues that it should instead see itself as a young country with its best days still ahead. Britain's attitude is contrasted with that of Brazil, a vibrant and dynamic emerging economy. Brazil has enjoyed a decade of prosperity, and its people display a fervent patriotic spirit, underpinned by a sense of optimism. A new 'baby boom', however, is ensuring that Britain, too, is a young and growing country. There are many promising opportunities for the future if the British are prepared to work hard.

We hope that these chapters, by identifying areas in which Britain can improve, will provoke some debate about our future as an advanced economy in the world. The world in 2012 offers exciting prospects for countries ready to seize the day. There is no reason why, following the example of other nations, Britain cannot share in this bright future.

1 The Chains

In the wake of the financial crisis, 1970s-style pessimism that Britain is destined to decline has returned. The British have lost confidence in themselves and in their history.

The Return of Decline

In March 1979, on the occasion of his retirement, the British Ambassador to Paris Sir Nicholas Henderson sent out the traditional valedictory letter to the Foreign Secretary. It was gloomy in tone. 'Our economic decline has been such as to sap the foundations of our diplomacy. Conversely, I believe that, during the same period, much of our foreign policy has been such as to contribute to that decline ... today we are not only no longer a world power, but we are not in the first rank even as a European one. Income per head in Britain is now, for the first time for over 300 years, below that in France.'[1]

The signs of this decline were everywhere:

> You only have to move about western Europe nowadays to realise how poor and unproud the British have become in relation to their neighbours. It shows in the look of our towns, in our airports, in our hospitals and in local amenities; it is painfully apparent in much of our railway system, which until a generation ago was superior to the continental one ... So far as the management of major capital projects by government is concerned our vision appears limited and our purpose changeable ... We started work on two large plans, the third London airport and the Channel tunnel, only to cancel both.[2]

Despite the apparent decline, some argued that there was something to be said for Britain's relative poverty. Perhaps it was the Germans and the French who worked too hard, while the Brits had discovered what really mattered: 'Others will argue that the British way of life, with ingenuity and application devoted to leisure rather than to work, is superior to that elsewhere and is in any case what people want.'[3] But as Henderson warned, it was doubtful that such a way of life could continue for long, if decline was continued.

By the time Henderson wrote his letter, Britain had arguably been in relative decline for nearly a hundred years. The former 'workshop of the world' had failed to take sufficient advantage of the second stage of the Industrial Revolution. The British lagged in developing chemicals behind Germany, in cars behind France and electricity behind America. In the wake of the 1929 Wall Street Crash and the worldwide Depression that followed, Britain retreated from its Victorian liberal principles.[4] The days of sound money, free trade and free competition were over. After the Second World War, the Government went still further, nationalising the health, gas, coal, and railway industries.

In 1950, Britain was still richer as a nation than France or West Germany. By the time of Henderson's letter, 30 years later, Britain had fallen behind. Between 1950 and 1973, Germany grew twice as fast per hour worked.[5] The long decades of uncompetitive markets and entrenched labour power had finally caught up with Britain. Economic weakness at home was matched by political weakness abroad. The Empire had disappeared. The debacle at Suez was evidence of a lack of influence, the relationship with America was weakened, and de Gaulle twice vetoed Britain's entrance into the Common Market. Britain could no longer be said to be a great power.

The 1970s would be seen as the nadir of British decline. British society was falling apart, as governments of both left and right found themselves squeezed between trade union power and growing inflation. Edward Heath had to declare an official State of Emergency a record five times in less than four years.[6] Unemployment passed 1 million in 1975, for the first time since the 1930s. Popular companies like Rolls Royce went bust. Frequent power cuts could bring the country to a standstill. Strikes and industrial disputes were endemic. Trade union leaders like Derek 'Red Robbo' Robinson, shop steward at British Leyland, proved as powerful as leading politicians. Between 1978 and 1979 he caused over 500 walk-outs at the Longbridge plant.[7] In hospitals, women gave birth by candlelight, traffic lights failed across the country,[8] and even Prime Minister's Questions was lit by candles and paraffin lamps.[9] *Blue Peter* taught children how to line blankets with newspaper to keep elderly relatives warm without heating. In early 1974, Britain was temporarily reduced to a three-day week. Rubbish piled up on the streets, and infamously during the 1978 so-called Winter of Discontent, even the dead were left unburied.

'Goodbye, Great Britain,' said a *Wall Street Journal* editorial, 'it was nice knowing you.'[10] 'Britain is a tragedy,' mourned Henry Kissinger. 'It has sunk to borrowing, begging, stealing until North Sea oil comes in.'[11] According to a Brussels correspondent, Britain was now only admired in Europe 'for its ability to stagger along on its knees'.[12] The dictator Idi Amin wrote to Heath offering aid, and claiming that he was 'following with sorrow the alarming economic crisis befalling on Britain'.[13]

In response to the crisis, British society turned inwards. Class divisions loomed large. As the foreign correspondent put it, 'The apparent fecklessness of the British worker and his delight in wringing the once golden goose's neck is matched in continental eyes by the reluctance of the British management to get to work first [and] roll up its sleeves.'[14] Trade unions and political parties became more radical, the political consensus of the postwar years broken.

Across the Western world, there was a sense that progress and growth was coming to an end. *The Limits to Growth*, written by a team of MIT researchers, published in 1972, argued that humanity's food and resources would soon run out. By 1992, the authors predicted, world supplies of zinc, gold, tin, copper and oil could be exhausted.[15] Within the decade, it had sold 4 million copies.[16] The 1967 *Famine, 1975!* warned that 'Population-food collision is inevitable; it is foredoomed.' Haiti, Egypt and India were already a lost cause, and should be left to starve.[17] The 1968 *The Population Bomb* argued that 'in the 1970s and 1980s, hundreds of millions of people will starve to death in spite of any crash programs embarked upon now. At this late date nothing can prevent a substantial increase in the world death rate.'[18] This apocalyptic book went on to sell 2 million copies.[19]

Clearly, the mass doom failed to come about. World populations continued to grow, and there is no sign yet of reaching a limit to resources. Britain, too, found its way back from the edge. Margaret Thatcher's reforms helped reintroduce competition back into the economy, and weakened trade union power. Between 1995 and 2007, UK real GDP per hour grew faster than France, Germany and even the United States.[20] The collapse of the Soviet Union in 1989 and the defeat of the Argentine military junta in 1982 helped regain international respect. Even British soft power recovered as culture boomed. For a brief moment in the mid 1990s it was possible to speak of 'Cool Britannia' without any apparent irony.

Yet, in the wake of the financial crisis of 2007, it seems that a spirit of decline has returned. 'Forget the Great in Britain', said an article in *Newsweek* in 2009.[21] Perhaps, people wondered, Margaret Thatcher didn't so much save Britain as put off the inevitable. The financial crisis showed, some argued, that the perceived prosperity of the 1980s was little more than a massive stock bubble. The quagmire of the Iraq War put to an end the idea of justified military intervention. Britain is increasingly isolated from the European Union, and distant from an America preoccupied by the rising BRIC (Brazil, Russia, India, China) economies. The prospects for long-term economic growth look gloomy. The national debt is above £1 trillion and growing.

The other symptoms of decline seem to have also returned. Radical political views are gaining support. Agonised navel-gazing is now the fashion, debating the distribution of growth, rather than how to grow the economy as a whole. Hundreds camped in the 'Occupy London' protests outside St Paul's Cathedral in the autumn of 2011. The West as a whole looks set to drastically shrink in influence compared to China and the other new economies. Once again, the idea that growth is unsustainable is popular. 'Every society clings to a myth by which it lives', argues Tim Jackson of the Sustainable Development Commission. 'Questioning growth is deemed to be the act of lunatics, idealists and revolutionaries. But question it we must. The myth of growth has failed us.' Instead, Jackson argues, we should focus on the 'quality of our lives and in the health and happiness of our families ... the strength of our relationships and our trust in the community'.[22] Even the three-day working week is seemingly back in fashion. The new economics foundation (nef) argues that instituting a 21-hour working week would help tackle 'overwork, unemployment, over-consumption, high carbon emissions, low well-being, [and] entrenched inequalities'.[23]

Britain has lost confidence in itself, and what it stands for. Britain once ruled the Empire on which the sun never set. Now it can barely keep England and Scotland together. No wonder many have concluded that we would do better to accept a gentle retirement, and spend more time relaxing in the garden.

Countries that are more confident in turn take more risks, make more investments, discover more inventions, and are more respected on the world stage. They look to compete with the best in the world, rather than give in to internal squabbling or defeatism. Perhaps the greatest achievement of Thatcher's administration was less taking on the unions or liberalising the economy, but making Britain believe in itself again.

Many of the world's democratic, liberal and free market institutions derive their origins in Britain, and we should be proud of that. British values helped created the modern world. Britain once prided itself on the virtues of responsible finance, public education, hard work, risk taking and ambition. It helped spread those ideas to the world – but now seems to have lost sight of many of them itself.

For much of the postwar era, there has been a damaging belief that economic growth is not really determined by effort. Other factors are regarded as being important: the structure of corporations or the way the money supply is operated. Unfortunately, this view actually harmed worked by diminishing their motivation. The draining of effort from our psyche has been replaced by a sense of entitlement. It has also led to a false belief in the value of industrial policy. Britain could avoid decline if only it could discover the 'magic formula' that leads other countries to success.

Of course, underlying the British faith in destiny is its class system. Although some argue that class is no longer a factor, a comparison of social mobility puts Britain near the bottom in the Western world.[24] Yet the suggested cures to this disease – abolishing grammar schools or redistributing wealth – have been, if anything, counterproductive. This is not just a problem of the left, however. Right-wing commentators are apt to argue about natural ability and talent, as if success is solely a result of destiny rather than persistence.

It is not surprising that this narrative has meant that Britons were ill-equipped to deal with the rising challenge of emerging economies, whose central cultural belief was that anyone could better themselves through education and hard work.

To avoid the decline, Britain needs to look out to rest of the world and learn once again what it seems to have forgotten.

2 A Tale of Two Nations

At the turn of the millennium, British voters and politicians demanded far more spending than they were prepared to raise in tax. The result was chronic deficits, and a country unprepared for the financial crisis. Across the Atlantic, Canada took a very different path.

It all seemed very different at the turn of the millennium. At the height of the dot com boom Britain could do no wrong. Its flexible economy flourished, easily outpacing the performance of our European neighbours. Never before had the country been so rich. New Labour could afford to pour record investment into public services, all paid for by taxes from world leading financial services. Waiting lists for hospitals continued to drop. Pupils seemed to set new exam records every year.

Then the bust arrived like another ice age. The boom, it was revealed, had been fuelled by credit card binges. British banks only survived through record Government bailouts. Spending on public services proved to be unsustainable. In any case, little of the extra money of the last ten years seemed to have been wisely spent. Even the exam results seemed unreliable, as suspicions of grade inflation grew. Britain's education performance, according to more rigorous world rankings, continued to slide each year.

It isn't hard to paint a worrying picture for the future of the UK. Its economy is stagnating, and doubts remain whether our political system has the will to truly tackle our debt. If the wealth of Britain's financial services is little more than a mirage, it is difficult to see where future growth will come from. Every attempt to reform public services is defeated by more determined special interests. As a small country, it seems inevitable that Britain will be squeezed between the might of the US and the growing Asian giants. The only alternative, the increasingly dysfunctional Eurozone, is hardly an attractive option.

It seems doubtful whether British students can ever compete with the Asian work ethic.

The fundamentals of the UK, this argument goes, are weak, and thus we are doomed to relative decline. There is little we as a nation or our politicians can do about it.

The problem with this startling nihilistic vision is the example of Canada.

It is easy to miss the similarities between the UK and Canada. On first glance at a map, the two countries seem very different. Canada is half the population of the UK (around 30 million), but immense in land mass. The UK is just under 100,000 square miles in size, whereas Canada is over 38 times larger, the second largest country in the world.[1] Whereas the UK has a gentle physical environment, Canada contains vast forests, volcanoes, much of the world's fresh water and the immense Arctic wastes. Canadians are richer than Britons. In 2010, GDP per capita was $46,200 in Canada, around a quarter higher than the UK's $36,400.

Compared to their similarities however, these differences are trivial. Both are small, first world, open economies. Both have their own currencies, but depend for their prosperity on trade with larger neighbours. Both countries share much of a common heritage: the same language, the same monarch and similar political institutions. Both like to think of themselves as the best friend of the United States. Life expectancy in both is around 80 years, with the average age half that.

The fundamentals of the UK and Canada, then, are largely similar. But their respective reactions to the financial crisis could not have been more different.

In Canada, none of the five major banks failed. While its economy was not completely immune from the global downturn, it comfortably rebounded, easily suffering least of the G7. Canadian deficits increased, but they did not grow out of control.

The future looks promising as well. The Canadian economy is among the strongest and freest in the world. Taxes are relatively low, but the Government still provides necessities such as universal healthcare. Canadian students are among the best in the world in terms of exam results.

How did Canada do so well for itself? Where did the UK go wrong? Could the UK have followed the same path?

The truth is that the Canadian economy has not always done so well. In fact, 20 years ago, it faced a financial crisis of its own.

How Canada Survived the Financial Crisis

In the early 1990s the Canadian economy was in trouble. Unemployment was high, growth was low and debt continued to grow. The *Wall Street Journal* joked about the 'Canadian Peso' and claimed Canada as 'an honorary member of the Third World'.[2]

Despite repeated attempts, governments seemed incapable of getting a grip on its deficit. Canadian debt had been high ever since the Second World War, but the deficit was largely under control until the premiership of Pierre Elliot Trudeau.

Trudeau was a fascinating character, a politician who liked to drive sports cars and dated celebrities such as Barbra Streisand. He was an excellent swimmer and diver, and even practised judo.[3] As a travelling youth his adventures included being thrown into a Jordanian jail as a Jewish spy, observing conflicts in India, Pakistan and Indochina, and escaping Shanghai just before it fell to Mao Zedong's Communists.

A lifelong believer in left-wing and Keynesian economics, his Master's dissertation at Harvard, never completed, was on the relationship between Communism and Catholicism. Subsequently he transferred to the London School of Economics to study under the Marxist economist Harold Laski.[4] He shared Laski's beliefs in greater state involvement in the economy, and that the West should seek reconciliation with the Soviet Union.

Trudeau would get the chance to put his big governments into action once in power. Over the course of his near 16-year rule, he succeeded in increasing the size of the state by a third, to 22.9 per cent of GDP. He ran deficits for all but one year, and by the time he left power in 1984 these had grown to over 8 per cent of GDP.[5] These deficits were mostly structural.[6] This meant that they would not simply disappear once the economy left behind recession.

At the time, few recognised the severity of the problem. Polls taken at the time showed that just 2 per cent of the population thought debt and deficits were the country's largest economic problem.[7] After all, in the Keynesian view of the time, deficits were necessary to support the wider economy. Canadian debt still remained comparatively low in international terms. In 1974, it had been just 18 per cent of GDP.[8]

Trudeau's liberals were replaced by the right-wing Progressive Conservatives, led by Brian Mulroney. Unlike Trudeau, Mulroney had a much more traditional background for a politician. He was born in 1939 to Catholic parents in the remote Quebec town of Baie-Comeau, one of six children. At university Mulroney became interested in politics, and won success as a member of the debating team. He became a youth delegate for the Progressive Conservatives, and soon managed to strike up a friendship with John Diefenbaker, who in 1957 became Canada's 13th Prime Minister. Like Diefenbaker, Mulroney admitted to dreaming of political leadership from an early age. Alongside his burgeoning political career, Mulroney sought a job in the law as well. He only passed his bar on the third attempt, but his firm kept him on because of his charm. As a labour lawyer Mulroney would win the public's attention through the televised Cliche Commission of 1974, helping to uncover corruption, violence and Mafia infiltration in the construction industry. Nevertheless, after losing an earlier leadership battle in 1976 to party rival Joe Clark, he retreated to the business world. He proved a success as Executive Vice President of the Iron Ore Company of Canada, and as Clark's popularity fell Mulroney took his chance to regain political power.

Mulroney represented a partial break with Canada's Keynesian past. He introduced more market-friendly ideas. He was Canada's Thatcher or Reagan, although never quite as successful. His main achievement was opening up the Canadian company and making it easier for Canadian business to trade with the world. He signed a free trade agreement with the United States in 1987, which would eventual lead to the signing of NAFTA (the North American Free Trade Agreement) in 1992. He significantly restructured the tax system, replacing the export-hitting Manufacturers' Sales Tax with a more transparent Goods and Services Tax. He privatised some of the state's crown corporations, and liberalised the energy sector. While these and other reforms supported Canada's later success, they unfortunately distracted attention from dealing with the deficit.

To his credit Mulroney did succeed in getting some control of the public finances, turning an operating deficit of 1.2 per cent of GDP into a surplus of 0.3 per cent by the time he left office.[9] A painful set of reforms and tax increases had at least ensured that, excluding the cost of the debt, Canada was no longer spending more than its taxes were bringing in.

But it was already too late. The debt level was simply too high, and investors were growing nervous. By this time, interest rates on ten-year bonds were near 10 per cent, almost twice as high as the growth rate of the Canadian economy. Canada had to run faster just to keep still. Debt continued to grow far faster than Canada could pay it down. Over the course of Mulroney's term from 1984 to 1993 debt grew from 46.9 per cent to 67 per cent of GDP.[10] At one point, 36 per cent of the taxes of the citizens in Ottawa was going towards paying off the national debt.[11] Even worse, the higher interest rates were slowing the economy, making it still harder to pay off the debt.

The situation was clearly getting out of control. The 1994 Mexican Peso Crisis had shown how quickly international investors could lose faith in a country. Unless Canada acted soon, it too faced the danger of the vicious cycle of falling investor confidence, increased debt and economic stagnation. By 1995 Canada's federal debt was 68.4 per cent of GDP. On top of this, it also faced provincial debt of 27.6 per cent of GDP.[12] As a whole, the Canadians' debt had passed an ominous 90 per cent of GDP.

With plunging approval ratings Mulroney resigned in 1993, to be replaced by Canada's first female Prime Minister, Kim Campbell. Born in 1947, Campbell found herself in the public gaze from any early age as a child host and reporter for the 1957 CBC programme *Junior Television Report*. Evidently deciding that the media wasn't for her, when she grew up she instead chose a career in academia and then politics.

In her 1993 election campaign, Campbell was admired for her frank honesty. Unfortunately, this honesty backfired when she revealed to journalists that neither the deficit nor unemployment were likely to be much reduced before the 'end of the century'.[13]

All the major parties promised spending cuts in the 1993 election. Campbell's Progressive Conservatives promised to eliminate the deficit within five years, while the more radical Reform Party pledged to do so within three. The Liberal Party by contrast, now under the leadership of Jean Chrétien and Finance Minister Paul Martin, pledged to reduce the deficit to 3 per cent of GDP.

By now, the Canadian public had woken up to the scale of the problem, and polls showed that tackling the deficit was the number-one priority.[14] There had now been three attempts to tackle the deficit since the 1980s, each of which had proved ultimately unsuccessful. Out of the G7, Canada's economic performance was the worst in the first half of the 1990s.[15] Even the Bank of Canada was warning of a dangerous debt spiral.

The Progressive Conservatives were annihilated in the September election, losing 99 per cent of their seats.[16] The Canadian public had lost faith in their ability to manage the economy. The Reform Party did well, winning 52 seats, but the new winner of the election was Chrétien's Liberals, with 177 seats.

It was to be the unlikely duo of left-wing Chrétien and Martin who were eventually to tackle the deficit. The two of them were to dominate Canadian politics for the next decade in a story that was to strangely mirror the relationship of Blair and Brown across the Atlantic. Chrétien was a popular, charismatic Prime Minister. Martin was known equally for his supposed economic competence and his pursuit of his leader's job. After finally achieving his goal of the leadership in 2003, he served a short and largely disastrous term in office where he became widely mocked as 'Mr Dithers' for his inability to make a decision.

There was of course one crucial difference between the record of Blair and Brown, and that of Chrétien and Martin. While Blair and Brown's legacy to Britain was a record deficit, Chrétien and Martin succeeded in eliminating Canada's.

Chrétien and Martin were fortunate in that the major political resistance they faced to their deficit reduction programme was internal. Their right-wing opposition, the Reform Party, was pushing, if anything, for them to go further.

This gave the Liberals the space to be radical. As Martin would become well known for saying, they would close the deficit 'come hell or high water'.[17] He was determined to avoid the 'quicksand of compound interest' and argued that 'the debt and deficit are not inventions of ideology'.[18]

Fortunately for Martin, he would succeed with what would come to be seen as a classic example of a fiscal contraction. Altogether, the Government cut federal spending by around 20 per cent between 1992 and 1997.[19]

The central feature of the Canadian approach was a comprehensive 'Programme Review'. Every area of Government spending was examined. For each programme, a team of ministers and civil servants examined whether the initiative was truly worth doing and, if so, whether it could be better done at a provincial level or within the private sector. If individual ministers couldn't come forward with sensible proposals, the Prime Minister threatened to impose 10 per cent cuts for them.

The strategy was to rethink what the Government did, rather than just make short-term adjustments that would quickly be reversed in years to come. Trying simply to slow the growth of spending had been attempted before, but it had failed. Absolute cuts were now needed.

At the same time, it was important that every department shared some of the pain. As Marcel Massé, the senior civil servant who led the review, said, 'There was blood on the floor everywhere, but at least everyone could see that others were hurting too.'[20] Even the health and veterans departments were to see moderate cuts.

Altogether, the Government made six to seven dollars of spending cuts to every dollar in new taxes.[21] The Government fired 45,000 civil servants, and slashed subsidies to business, agriculture and the regions.[22] The rates and the eligibility for unemployment insurance were reduced. Petro-Canada, a Government-owned energy company, was sold. Airports were transferred to localities and the railway CN sold. Transport spending fell by 50 per cent, while the defence budget was cut by 15 per cent.[23]

Welfare proved to be one of the main sources of savings. Canada's Unemployment Insurance allowed citizens to claim for up to 50 weeks after just ten weeks of work. In some seasonal industries such as fishing, some workers settled into an annual routine of two months of work, followed by ten months 'on the pogey'.[24] By 1999, Martin's reforms had ensured that the total paid out in unemployment benefits was 40 per cent less in real terms than in 1990. Far fewer people could qualify.[25]

Treasury forecasts were kept deliberately cautious, much more pessimistic than those of the private sector. The actual results exceeded everyone's expectations. Canada ran a surplus for every year between 1997 and 2009. The result was that federal debt fell from 67 per cent to only 29 per cent of GDP.[26] Despite the fiscal contraction, there was little effect on the wider economy. Between 2001 and 2007, the Canadian economy grew at the same rate as the British, at 2.6 per cent.

The real test of the economy's durability, however, was to come with the 2007 financial crisis. Canada couldn't avoid the impact of the crisis entirely: the main customer for its exports, after all, was the troubled US. Nevertheless, Canada rebounded faster than any other member of the G7. Part of the reason was that Canada had the room to indulge in fiscal stimulus when the economic recession arrived. Canada had, to steal a phrase, rebuilt its roof while the sun was shining. Net debt in 2008 was just 22 per cent of GDP.[27]

Debt Delusion?

Writing in 1849, the famous Whig historian Lord Macaulay complained, 'At every stage in the growth of [the national] debt the nation has set up the same cry of anguish and despair. At every stage in the growth of that debt it has been seriously asserted by wise men that bankruptcy and ruin were at hand. Yet still the debt kept on growing; and still bankruptcy and ruin were as remote as ever ...'[28]
His diagnosis is telling as that of any modern economist:

> They erroneously imagined that there was an exact analogy between the case of an individual who is in debt to another individual and the case of a society which is in debt to a part of itself ... They were under an error not less serious touching the resources of the country. They made no allowance for the effect produced by the incessant progress of every experimental science, and by the incessant efforts of every man to get in on life. They saw that the debt grew; and they forgot that other things grew as well as the debt.[29]

One hundred and fifty years later, many commentators were still playing the same tune. Economist Paul Krugman complains of widespread 'deficit panic'[30] and that attempts to cut Britain's current deficit are no better than a 'medieval doctor bleeding his patient'.[31] 'If we are bust today', argued journalist Johann Hari, then 'We were bust when we beat the Nazis. We were bust when we built the NHS.'[32] The idea that the UK is in a deficit crisis is 'the biggest lie in British politics'. *New Statesman* Political Editor Medhi Hasan wrote a book in 2011 debunking the supposed ten myths of 'debt delusion'.
Economists, from both left and right, echo Macaulay in complaining that it is misleading to compare the national debt to the debt of a

household. 'Since my undergraduate days, I have been pointing out that a government budget is not the same as that of an individual or company', protests journalist Samuel Brittan, 'The message is still too counterintuitive to get across.'[33] Commenting on the British Prime Minister's use of the metaphor of growing credit card bills, economist David Blanchflower argues that this is 'Asinine nonsense ... Cameron is an economic simpleton.'[34]

Behind these arguments lie two fundamentally different economic interpretations, often left undistinguished. The first notes only that there is after all, in Adam Smith's phrase, a great deal of ruin in a nation. A nation is indeed not the same thing as a household: it grows steadily richer with each passing decade, it can print its own money, and can be expected to live, more or less, forever. A nation can afford immense debts that would be crippling to any other institution, and pay them off at a leisurely pace.

But the second argument says something fundamentally different, and far stronger. Under this point of view, debt not only poses less of a danger to a nation, it doesn't matter *at all*. It is a residual, the simple counterpart of the wider economy's saving.

'Look after unemployment', economist John Maynard Keynes once said in a radio interview, 'and the budget will take care of itself.' Under one interpretation of Keynesian thought, unemployment is all that matters. 'Countries don't go bust', claimed former Citibank chairman Walter Wriston.[35] What may initially look like a debt crisis, goes the argument, is just a lack of confidence in future growth. Increase growth any way you can, even through greater deficits now, and the debt will decrease itself.

A quick examination of the history of the British debt might give some grounds for this easy complacency. Ever since its first creation in the late seventeenth century, the British debt has followed a simple pattern. It has spiked dramatically with every war, and then gradually been paid back down in the years of peace that followed. By the end of the Napoleonic wars debt had peaked at 268 per cent of GDP.[36] The long peace that followed gave Britain enough room to pay down the debt, until by 1914 it was only 26 per cent of GDP.[37] The two world wars took debt back up to 250 per cent of GDP. This was once again paid down, until in 2001 debt stood at 29.7 per cent of GDP. Even after the financial crisis, the UK's debt is expected to peak at no more than around 80 per cent of GDP in 2015.[38]

The trajectory of the debt seems to bear little relationship to the short-term deficit. Throughout the nineteenth century, Chancellors of the Exchequer ran near perfectly balanced budgets. From 1830 to 1913, the UK budget deficit averaged near 0 per cent. The UK ran a deficit of greater than 1 per cent of GDP in only four years between 1816 and 1899. In the twentieth century, by contrast, the Government ran almost constant deficits after the Second World War. Between 1950 and 1987, the Government ran a deficit in all but three years.

Nevertheless, debt fell, if anything, faster in the twentieth century than it did in the nineteenth. As Macaulay suggested, the growth of debt can only ever really be judged in comparison to the growth of the economy as a whole. Keep either growth or inflation high enough and perhaps a Government can run a deficit for perpetuity, while still seeing its debt shrink.

Or can it?

If it is really is impossible for countries to go bust, then it is strange that so many countries have failed to pay back their loans. From Edward III defaulting on his loans to Florence financiers in 1340[39] through to today's Eurozone crisis, sovereign defaults have been a constant feature throughout history. In their definitive text, *This Time is Different*, economists Carmen M. Reinhart and Kenneth S. Rogoff list hundreds of examples of default through the last 800 years. Default is not just not unknown, it is endemic. Only a small number of countries – such as Australia, New Zealand, Canada, Denmark, Thailand and the United States[40] – have never defaulted. The UK has been relatively fortunate in past centuries, but it too defaulted. In 1340 Edward III betrayed his Florence creditors and Charles II stopped the Exchequer in 1672, bankrupting many of the leading creditors.

It turns out that a country's budget is not so far away from a household budget, after all. Run up unsustainable debts, and eventually people will stop wanting to lend you money. Theoretically a country can pay off any debts through increased taxes or simply printing money. In practice, democratic anger and uncontrollable hyperinflation make that difficult. Throughout the ages, sovereigns have discovered that it is far easier to simply stop paying than try to squeeze more revenue out of an overtaxed population. Historian Niall Ferguson has suggested a rule of thumb that when debt service reaches 20 per cent of a sovereign's revenue, nations have found it easier to default.[41]

That is not to say that defaulting on your debt is costless. In the short run, defaulting on debt generally leads to loss of confidence, recession and plummeting currency values. Mexico's default in the early 1980s led to a 'lost decade' that affected much of Latin America. In the long run, it can take decades to regain the trust of international investors. In the meantime interest rates will remain stubbornly high as investors seek to hedge themselves against the risk of your defaulting in the future. Britain was immensely helped in its wars against Napoleon and France by its capability to borrow much greater funds. At that time, investors had much more faith in its institutional ability to pay the money back eventually.

Even if a country pays the interest on its debts, the fear of default can lead to high interest rates from worried investors. One study suggested that a 20 per cent rise in the proportion of US debt to GDP would leave the country facing interest rates 0.2–1.2 per cent higher.[42] Higher interest rates in turn 'crowd out' private investment. In the long run, these higher rates hurt the underlying health and growth rate of the economy. As growth rates compound over the time scales of decades, even small differences can have immense effects. Over a century, a country that grows at 2 per cent rather than 1 per cent will end up 2.5 times as rich. The danger is that, in the words of former economic advisor to President Obama, Christina Romer, 'Such crowding out may have enormous effects on standards of living over a century, but are unlikely to be noticeable over a decade or two.'[43]

The most notorious attempt to quantify this effect comes, again, from economists Reinhart and Rogoff. They looked at the relationship between debt and growth in 44 countries over the last 200 years. The top quarter of the worst offenders, those whose debt was over 90 per cent of GDP, found growth slowed significantly. The average slowdown was 1 per cent, but the unlucky saw growth slow by 4 per cent and worse.[44] A 2010 paper for the IMF by economists Manmohan S. Kumar and Jaejoon Woos discovered that a 10 per cent increase in the debt-to-GDP ratio leads to a 0.2 per cent slowdown in the growth rate. Again, there were particularly bad effects once debt passed above 90 per cent of GDP.[45] Countries with high public debts seem to invest less, and eventually this makes their workers less productive.

Reinhart and Rogoff also found that a single financial crisis causes government debt to spike on average by 86 per cent over the following three years.[46] Financial crises, while rare, are a fact of life. In that sense any nation, even those with low levels of debt, are at risk of passing the dangerous 90 per cent debt-to-GDP threshold.

In this case, it is tempting to move from the comfortable complacency over 'debt delusion' to despair that trying to control the budget is hopeless. Why make the difficult sacrifices to keep a budget in surplus and risk enduring public unpopularity when a financial crisis can undermine all fiscal stability anyway? To misquote Keynes, voters can remain irrational longer than you can remain in power.

The problem with this view is that deficits do matter, even in the short term, even ignoring entirely their effects on the total debt. While Government debt continued to fall throughout the second half of the twentieth century, the public finances were far from continually healthy.

Run a deficit, and you run the risk of promoting inflation and unsustainable booms in the economy. Government deficits might add demand to an economy, but more demand isn't always a good thing. If you run a deficit, you will allow public spending to grow unsustainably with little checks to make sure that the public are getting good value for money. When the inevitable crash comes, a spendthrift Government will soon discover that it is a lot easier to hand out goodies than to take them back again.

Economists used to believe that the high inflation of the 1970s was the result of the oil shocks, an outside emergency that no Government could ever have avoided. We now know that an equally significant cause were Governments themselves, desperately trying to boost economies by increasing deficits beyond what was sustainable.

The 1950s and 1960s were a golden age for Western economies. Growth has never been as fast since. Eventually this boom faded, but Western policy-makers were reluctant to accept just how much growth had slowed. During the postwar years, the underlying growth in Western economies averaged 3 per cent a year. By the early 1970s, it had slowed to as little as 1.5 per cent a year.[47]

Rather than accept the new reality and work for long-term growth, governments tried to stimulate their economies through ever greater deficits and inflation. The late 1960s were the height of debt-delusion Keynesianism. Policy-makers truly believed that they could spend their way to lower unemployment. As long as higher growth was achieved, deficits would take care of themselves. In his last budget, President Kennedy argued that 'The choice ... is between chronic deficits arising out of a slow rate of economic growth, and temporary deficits stemming from a tax program designed to promote fuller use of our resources and more rapid economic growth.'[48]

The deficit plan didn't work. Growth only increased again in the 1980s, long after the Keynesian strategy had been abandoned. Inflation rose in the US from 1 per cent at the beginning of the Kennedy administration to over 5 per cent at the end of the 1960s, and 10 per cent over the course of the 1970s. In the UK inflation averaged 13 per cent in the 1970s, peaking as high as 25 per cent in 1975.

It turns out that debt does matter. Government spending has to be responsible, or an economy will suffer in both the short and the long run. Governments that lose control of their finances eventually lose control of their own destiny.

In 1976, reflecting back on the failed experiment of the Keynesian decades, Labour Prime Minister Jim Callaghan famously confessed that 'We used to think that you could spend your way out of a recession and increase employment by cutting taxes and boosting government spending. I tell you in all candour that that option no longer exists.'[49]

Twenty years later, another Labour Government would come to power, determined not to repeat the mistakes of previous years. Prudence was to be the watchword. Discipline and caution would be the guiding principles.

How, then, did the New Labour Government of Tony Blair and Gordon Brown end up leaving the country quite so unprepared for the financial storm that was eventually to burst?

The Prudent Chancellor

In December 1992, a young leader writer for the *Financial Times* wrote a paper for the Fabian Society, criticising the then Exchange Rate Mechanism, and warning of the dangers of any future European Monetary Union. The author believed that the dangers of losing economic flexibility were too great. By letting 'economic schemes run ahead of political realities' the EMU risked 'destroying rather than cementing European political ties and undermining rather than propelling European economic and political integration'.[50]

More to the point, the paper argued that there were better ways to gain credibility and seek stability. Control of monetary policy could be passed over to an independent Bank of England, ensuring that politicians could no longer interfere. New fiscal rules could reassure the markets that the Government wasn't about to run up unsustainable debts, while leaving enough room for the Government to respond to a downturn when needed. If implemented correctly, such policies could see an end to boom and bust.

The failure of the Exchange Rate Mechanism that year had created space for new ideas, but also significant problems for the two main political parties. While the Conservatives may have received the public's blame for the disaster eventually culminating in Black Wednesday, new Shadow Chancellor Gordon Brown was only too aware that his party had been in favour of the ERM as well. He needed a new economic policy, and fast. The young journalist seemed to offer it. Brown dropped a line to the editor of the *Financial Times*, and asked if it would be possible to set up a meeting with the writer, a certain Edward Balls.

Ed Balls was born in 1967 in Norwich, the first child of parents Michael and Carolyn. Ed was clearly very influenced by the hard work of his father Michael, who after earning a scholarship to the local grammar school went on to study at Keble College, Oxford, and then started his academic career in the US. He would go on to become both an internationally renowned zoologist, dedicated to finding alternatives to animal testing, and a keen Labour activist. Ed, too, worked very hard at his schooling, doing well at the private Nottingham High,[51] and then taking a good First in PPE during his Keble years. After a few months at the Treasury in 1989, he earned a Kennedy Memorial Scholarship to Harvard.

Harvard at the time was at the centre of 'New Keynesianism', the fashionable school of thought of the day. It would go on to provide much of the intellectual backing for Clinton's New Democrats. Balls' teacher Larry Summers later went on to become Secretary of the Treasury under President Clinton and Director of the National Economic Council for President Obama. In the late 1980s, he had written an influential paper arguing for the benefits of independent central banks. Other influences at Harvard included Lawrence Katz, who became chief economist at the Labour Department, and Robert Reich who served as Secretary of Labour.[52] Much of their thought could still be seen in New Labour's later minimum wage and New Deal initiatives.

Returning back to the UK, Balls took the job as a journalist at the *Financial Times* where he later caught the attention of Gordon Brown. At first, he was unsure whether to take the position (and the lower salary) of working for Brown, and asked his journalist friends for advice: Martin Wolf of the *Financial Times* thought he should turn it down, William Keegan of the *Observer* told him to go for it, while Will Hutton of the *Guardian* could not decide.[53] It was only when his newspaper refused his request to spend a couple of years in Africa that he finally made his mind up.

Brown, too, had worked hard as a pupil, and soon found himself drawn to academia and journalism. Part of an experimental fast-track scheme at his Kirkcaldy High School, Brown had completed his A Levels and gone on to the University of Edinburgh by 16. He would soon become editor of the student newspaper, and after university would go on to become the current affairs editor for Scottish Television. Unlike Balls, however, Brown's intellectual interests were less in middle-of-the-road Keynesian liberalism, and more in traditional socialist history and thought. For his doctoral research he looked at the development of Labour Party politics in Scotland in the 1920s, while he went on in 1975 to edit *The Red Paper on Scotland*. Its authors demanded a state-planned economy, nationalisation of industry and the destruction of the ruling class. It was only later in the 1980s that Brown began his transition to the mainstream of economic thought.

Nevertheless, as future students of his budget speeches soon recognised, Brown's real interests always laid in micro measures, tinkering with subsidies and benefit levels. What Ed Balls offered him was a comprehensive programme for stability, a state of the art New Keynesian policy machine straight from Harvard. Put in place a technocratic system of regulation, and the markets would leave you alone with enough discretion to pursue your real passions.

Gordon Brown came of age in the 1960s when Anthony Crosland's *The Future of Socialism* was the dominant intellectual force in British politics. In particular, Crosland believed that private enterprise could be used for social ends by controlling management. There was no need for nationalisation when the state could get its way through other means. This was a precursor to Gordon Brown's 'prawn cocktail corporatism' where big business, especially in the City, operated under license from the state in exchange for large slugs of cash which could then be poured into public services and wealth redistribution. Rather than making the difficult decisions to improve the capability of the individual, this view simply assumed a growing pie in which the only policy decision was how to cut shares in it.

Over the next five years, Balls and Brown continued to develop their macroeconomic system. By March 1995, as the New Labour elite held an all day retreat at the seventeenth-century Fritham hunting lodge in the New Forest, Balls was presenting to Tony Blair and Brown on his new 22-page policy paper, 'The Macroeconomic Framework'.

Later, in 2002, Ed Balls and Gus O'Donnell[54] would proudly write up this framework into a 400-page book, *Reforming Britain's Economic and Financial Policy*. The authors hoped that the book would 'be of interest to economics students, undergraduates or postgraduates ... This book differs from traditional textbooks in that all the policies described here are actually being implemented. Hence there is much more detail on *how* to achieve certain objectives which those interested only in the theory might choose to skip.'[55]

Beyond students, the authors had another, less humble audience in mind. As Gordon Brown wrote in his introduction, 'this book makes clear that the prosperity brought about by the new macroeconomic framework is not just for Britain'.[56] The authors firmly believed that they had solved the problem of boom and bust. They were now ready to sell their instruction manual to the world.

At the heart of Balls' framework was prudence, a principle that appealed deeply to Gordon Brown and his Presbyterian self-image. Every past Government had found itself in trouble when growth and the deficit had turned out worse than earlier forecasts. Balls' new system would avoid this: prudent monetary policy would hand over control of interest rates to the central bank. At the same time, prudent fiscal rules would lead to sustainable spending in the long term. Brown and Balls would deliberately use conservative growth assumptions in planning their spending commitments. In the short term, Brown forbade other Labour ministers from making spending promises. For the first two years of the new Government, Brown would cap spending growth, matching the Conservative Chancellor Ken Clarke's tough budget plans.

Many commentators and more than a few politicians found themselves a little taken aback by Labour's newly found discipline. Ken Clarke later admitted that he probably wouldn't have stuck to his own targets, while most in the Treasury thought the pledges were little more than a 'clever wheeze'.[57] As Robert Peston argued in his 2006 biography, Brown was 'making an almost religious atonement for the sins of Labour's past. He put on a hairshirt and insisted the rest of the Party did too.'[58] Between 1997 and 2001, current spending grew at just 1.7 per cent, far below both the rate of spending growth during John Major's term or the 2.5 per cent growth of the economy as a whole. Investment, long an obsession of Brown, was at its lowest level since the 1970s.[59] In 2003, the *Observer* economics editor William Keegan wrote a book complaining that 'The Prudence of Mr Gordon Brown' was rather overdone.[60] Many wondered what had happened to the 'Red Gordon' of the 1970s who had argued so passionately for greater public control and spending. Some blamed the austere instincts of the ambitious Ed Balls, whom one profiler sarcastically suggested might perhaps be a 'closet Keynesian'.[61]

But then there was always a second stage to Brown and Ball's masterplan. Brown really did believe in transferring more money to the poor, more spending on the public services and increasing investment in infrastructure. Once credibility and trust had been won, then there would be an opportunity to increase spending again.

New Labour had always seen as part of its mission the task of raising investment in the public services, arguing they had been starved of funds during the Conservative years. The public sector didn't need reform to improve productivity – it just needed more money.

In 2000, the spending began. The growth rate of current spending was pushed up to 2.5 per cent a year. The NHS was granted a 6.1 per cent annual growth for four years, which the Treasury claimed to be a new record.[62] At the same time, the small-print of Gordon Brown's Golden Rule allowed him to ignore investment when judging the budget balance. Taking full advantage, Brown doubled net investment. In 2002, spending growth was speeded up again, to a projected 3.3 per cent between 2004 and 2006, well above the Treasury's estimates of the growth rate of the economy.[63] Journalist Philip Stephens described it as the moment the party finally chose social democracy.[64]

Gordon Brown's prudence was partially a response to memories of the chaos and irresponsibility of the 1970s. Equally traumatising were memories of Labour's surprise general election defeat in 1992. A good part of the reason for the defeat, the party's insiders felt, was that the voters had revolted against Neil Kinnock's 'tax bombshell'.

If Labour was ever to regain power, both Blair and Brown believed, it had to keep control of spending and promise never to raise taxes again.

It should have been obvious that pledges to spend more on the public services, not raise taxes and maintain prudent finances formed an impossible triangle. Something had to give. Ultimately it was the prudent finances that were abandoned.

In 2002, the most Balls and Brown felt they could electorally afford to raise taxes was a new 1 per cent increase in national insurance rates. Even this modest move made Blair nervous,[65] and the ground was carefully prepared. The independent Wanless report was commissioned – carefully designed to return the conclusion that the NHS was in need of greater resources.

It was clear from the Treasury's own forecasts that this would not be enough to close the gap in the Government's books. From 1998 to 2001, the Government had run a surplus. The 2002 budget forecast a growing deficit throughout the next five years,[66] but the Government believed it had a good excuse for this. The world economy was weak in the aftermath of 9/11 and the bursting of the dot com bubble. The whole purpose of the Golden Rule was to allow greater discretionary deficits in economic downturns; the Government could point to the surpluses it had already run since 1997. As long as its budget forecasts were reasonably accurate, Brown should meet his primary fiscal rule, to balance the budget 'over the course of the cycle'. Even Kenneth Rogoff, then the Chief Economist of the IMF, gave the plans his cautious approval.[67] He did, however, warn that deficits should not be allowed to rise above their currently forecast path.

The forecasts did not prove to be accurate. The Government's budget never moved back into structural surplus,[68] let alone ran an actual surplus. The Treasury's estimates proved systematically over-optimistic. Despite Brown and Ball's new textbook economic framework, their forecasts proved as badly off as those of their predecessors in the 1970s. The American economist Jeffrey Frankel studied the difference between forecasts and reality of growth for 33 countries. The UK proved one of the worst offenders. On average, its forecasts for three years in the future were too optimistic by 3 per cent. This 3 per cent margin of error was enough to let the Treasury confidently assume that if they didn't balance in today's budget, than they would in the next.[69] Needless to say, tomorrow never came.

Later, members of New Labour were to insist that that they had run a responsible fiscal policy, and that the sole cause of the deficit was the unforeseeable economic storm of the Great Recession. Yes, they had increased spending, but only as the public had demanded to tackle years of underinvestment.

Let's compare the path of the UK deficit to the choices made by other countries. Canada, Australia and Chile all ran a surplus between 2000 and 2008. Sweden and Switzerland ran surpluses from the middle of the decade, and their budgets stayed in structural surplus even through the financial crisis. They spent less than they earned. Perhaps it is inevitable that official forecasts will be overly optimistic – but Governments still have a responsibility to look at why earlier predictions were wrong, and to try and put things right.

By contrast, the end of Balls and O'Donnell's 2002 vainglorious economics instruction manual, after giving itself a glowing report for 'success in ... low and stable inflation ... sound public finances ... economic stability', somewhat ominously finishes with the assurance, 'Nevertheless, both the Government and the [Monetary Policy Committee] recognise that it is important not to be complacent.'[70] Yet this is precisely what they failed to do.

Instead, Ed Balls and Gordon Brown depended solely on their own system, believing everything would be fine as long as they remained true to the increasingly contorted letter of the law. Doubts about investment and the use of off balance sheet financial vehicles began to grow. In 2005 the fiscal rule was only met by moving the start date of the current economic circle back two years from 1999 to 1997 – giving the Treasury two more years of surpluses to offset against the more recent deficits.

While Brown and Balls may have been in charge, the easy complacency about the British economy spread much further. There was little outcry from the other political parties or independent commentators in the media that Britain was spending too much. The gradual creep of extra regulation and extra barriers to growth wasn't seriously questioned. The British people were not exactly crying out for spending cuts or lower taxes.

Indeed, they were largely running up their own debts on credit, or withdrawing money from their mortgage. In a time when boom and bust had 'ended', and property prices only seemed to rise, there seemed little harm in indulging ever more on the credit card. On the eve of the crisis in 2007, total British personal debt passed GDP for the first time;[71] 18 per cent of British adults had more than £10,000 of unsecured debt.[72]

In 2008, the household savings ratio was the lowest it had been in 40 years, at just 1.7 per cent of household resources. It had used to average closer to 8 per cent.[73] Britain had seemingly forgotten the virtues of saving for tomorrow.

By January 2012, the average British adult owed £29,634, 122 per cent of average earnings (£26,000).[74] The total British debt, household and Government, is now around 492 per cent of GDP. That compares to just 282 per cent total debt for the US.[75] Of the world's major economies, only Japan is in anywhere near as bad a condition as Britain[76] – and Japan has suffered 20 years of economic stagnation.

Perhaps ironically, one of the few calls for fiscal responsibility came from left-wing commentator Polly Toynbee. Again and again, she argued in her *Guardian* column for greater public spending. Perhaps she was complacent about the real value that extra spending alone would bring – in 2003, she boasted, 'The NHS is the most efficient health system in the world: now it is well financed, it can be the best. Education is already sweeping up the OECD tables: improving at this rate, we shall reach top ratings.'[77]

Nevertheless, she recognised that any extra spending would have to be paid for. In 1999, she despaired, 'If this most popular government doesn't dare to start to change public attitudes on tax, no one will have so good a chance for many years to come. Tax by stealth has been rumbled, so now it is time for open advocacy. You only get what you pay for.'[78] In 2000, 'Taxation is fiscally virtuous because it allows spending without inflating the economy.'[79] In 2001, 'Long-term security for a left of centre government comes from persuading the public of the case for higher taxes – not from stealth or subterfuge.'[80] And then again, 'Not so long ago the chancellor's men would deny point blank what everyone knew: the price must be paid.'[81]

Few listened. Instead the British public and their Government went on spending on credit right until the bubble burst.

In 2007, the arrival of the financial crisis shattered the UK's finances, and, with them, Balls and Brown's system. In 2007, the fiscal rules were abandoned as tax revenues collapsed. The UK deficit moved into the double figures, while the UK suddenly found itself with one of the largest structural deficits in the G20. The latest estimates suggest that the UK economy is at least 13 per cent smaller than the authorities believed as recently as 2008.[82] Debt is projected to pass 70 per cent of GDP by 2015. In order to return back to any sort of budget balance, the UK faces seven hard years of spending cuts.

There were two very different kinds of response to the financial crisis. Some countries like Britain, or the US, or the Eurozone, found their old irresponsibility catching up with them. The financial crisis revealed huge holes in their future spending plans. The lifestyle of both private and public sectors in these countries was simply unsustainable. Then there were others, such as Sweden, Chile, Switzerland – or Canada – who had taken the opportunity of the good years to pay down their debts and reform their economies. Their budgets look set to return to surplus soon, growth has recovered, and the confidence of the markets remains strong.

On the other side of the world another Anglophone island shows a path Britain could have taken. Australia, like Britain, is a small, open and liberal economy.

Indeed, over the course of the twentieth century, Australia's economy followed a similar path to that of Britain and Canada. One of the wealthiest countries in the world at the beginning of the century, a succession of statist Governments eventually hurt the economy's underlying productivity and innovation. By the 1970s, the country had fallen far behind America, and growth had stagnated. In the 1980s, Paul Keating, at that time lead finance minister for the Labor Government, warned that the country was in danger of becoming a 'banana republic'. In response, he and Prime Minister Bob Hawke began an ambitious programme of reform: reducing trade barriers, privatising industries, and taking on the power of the trade unions. The cost of Australia's tariffs, the effective rate of protection for manufacturing, fell from 35 per cent in the 1970s to just 5 per cent by 2003.[83] Another of Keating's reforms, the creation of compulsory pension 'superannuation' accounts, means that nearly all Australian workers have their own private savings for retirement. Almost uniquely among Western nations, Australia's government has little financial reason to worry about the aging of its population.

Australia was more fortunate than Britain in that it did not run up nearly so much debt from the Second World War. Nevertheless, by the early 1990s the two countries were not so far from each other. In 1992, Australia's debt was 27 per cent of GDP, while the UK had 32 per cent. At the turn of the millennium, the debt of Australia and Britain was in a largely similar position. Over the next 15 years, the UK ran surpluses in just three years: 1999, 2000 and 2001. Meanwhile, under the leadership of Liberal Prime Minister John Howard, Australia ran surpluses every single year between 1997 and 2007. The result was that on the eve of the financial crisis, in 2007, Australia had just 9 per cent of debt compared to Britain's 44 per cent.[84]

Thanks to the stability 30 years of economic reform had granted it, Australia has thrived, barely affected by either the Asian crisis in the late 1990s or the worldwide recession in 2001. While the country benefited from its strong position in commodities, a larger reason was the legacy of continued reform. In 2007, sensible monetary and fiscal policy helped cushion the economy from the effects of the 2007 financial crisis. In late 2008 the Government could even afford to send out cheques for A\$900 to every taxpayer to help stimulate the economy.[85] Australia's four major banks held up well, avoiding the fate of British or American banks. Australia has now not suffered a recession since 1991, while growth has averaged 3.4 per cent in real terms.

Debt is never just about debt. It is a symptom of the irresponsibility that runs underneath, an attempt to enjoy more than one is prepared to pay for. Through history, governments and investors have found themselves in trouble when they have let their optimism run ahead of their caution. States have lost the faith of the markets when they have lost the ability to ability to tell their populations that they can't have everything now.

Debt crises are dangerous precisely because they arrive when their victims have become too complacent to prepare for them. It is not a coincidence that British growth now seems stagnant, debt is spiralling and the public sector has grown out of control. Governments that lose control of their spending lose control of their economy.

Leaving the crisis to one side, one could just about argue that Balls and Brown met the technocratic terms of their fiscal rule up until 2007. One could not argue that they had been prudent.

The 'Resilient' Economy

In 2008, the global financial system was in crisis. In the wake of the crash of the housing bubble, banks were being bailed out all over much of the Western world – everywhere, that is, but Canada.

None of the major Canadian banks failed. Canada didn't suffer a housing bubble or dangerous build-up of personal debt. In the years running up to the financial crisis, it ran a minor trade surplus. Indeed, it is hard to think of a more glowing report than the IMF gave in 2009: 'Through 2007, Canada experienced strong growth, price stability, fiscal and current account surpluses, historically low unemployment, and financial stability.' The reason for this success? The IMF credited 'strong fiscal discipline, sound and credible monetary policy, and robust financial supervision and regulation'. Even Canada's stimulus package was praised for being 'appropriately sized ... prudently based ... [and] with sizeable infrastructure spending and permanent tax cuts ... weighted toward items that are most effective in stimulating demand'.[86]

So why did Canada prove so resilient to the worldwide downturn?

One answer is that Canada enjoys a far more diversified economy than most other countries in the West. Although it enjoys a sizeable services sector, the country also owns important farming, manufacturing and energy industries. During the recession, the downturn in the rest of the economy was partially stabilised by the ongoing boom in commodities such as oil, gas and minerals. Continued demand from the growing Asian economies ensured that exports remained 50 per cent higher than during previous recessions.[87]

Another factor often pointed to is Canada's supposedly superior system of financial regulation. The Canadian banks are required to hold far higher amounts of capital than their British and American counterparts, protecting them better in the event of a sudden downturn. Canadians who take out a mortgage on more than 80 per cent of the value of the property are required to buy default insurance. Unlike in the US, mortgage interest can't be set against taxes, meaning there is more incentive to pay down your debt quickly. The five banks are banned from merging, and to some extent protected from foreign competitors, meaning that there is little incentive for risky competition. Even banker bonuses remain relatively low.

But while the story that Canada's success is down to better regulation is intuitively appealing, the reality is more complicated. In many ways, Canada has less regulation than the US. Canadian banks were never banned from interstate banking, or the union of retail and investment banking. The stability of Canadian banking is also old. Canada not only escaped a banking crisis in 2008, it also avoided a crisis in 1930 in the wake of the Wall Street crash. Earlier still, Canada was unaffected by the US banking panics of 1893 or 1930.[88]

There are five major Canadian banks: the Royal Bank of Canada, the Toronto Dominion Bank, the Bank of Nova Scotia, the Bank of Montreal and the Canadian Imperial Bank of Commerce. All five are located within a few hundred yards of each other in the skyscrapers of Bay Street, Toronto, not far from the shore of Lake Ontario.

Their strength seems to be less down to any particular set of rules than, as Finance Minister Jim Flaherty describes it, to its 'boring' culture.[89] In banking, it seems that there are clear advantages to being boring – a recent World Economic Forum report rated Canadian banks as the world's soundest.

At the head of the Canadian system is its chief regulator, a lifelong civil servant, Julie Dickson. Dickson is most described by those who know who her as quiet or reserved.[90] As Superintendent of the Office of the Superintendent of Financial Institutions (OSFI), she works from a sparse 23rd floor office, directly opposite the Toronto Stock Exchange. In interviews with journalists, she often argues that the ability to pick up the phone and make the right calls is far more important than ticking off any checklist.[91] Dickson is modest as well, recently refusing to allow a magazine to illustrate its profile of her with her photograph on the cover.

Canada opted out of much of the emphasis on securitisation and greater leverage that took over New York and London from the 1980s on. As other countries lowered their capital requirements, Canada raised its own. According to Finance Minister Flaherty, even Communist China once suggested that maybe Canadian banks were too timid.

The resilience of the Canadian economy was based on more than just the prudent culture of its banks. In 2006 the Liberal Party of Jean Chrétien and Paul Martin was finally thrown out after 13 years in office. They were replaced by a newly united Conservative Party and its leader Stephen Harper, although Harper would not achieve a majority government until 2011. For the most part, the Conservative Party's minority administrations did not stray too far from the path laid down by its Liberal predecessors. Canada maintained control of its finances, and made sure its economy remained friendly to growth.

No single measure can judge the freedom of an economy, but we can get some idea from composites which aggregate together many different factors of tax and regulation. Since 1995, the Heritage Foundation and the *Wall Street Journal* have published a composite index measuring the level of freedom in world economies. The freest country in 2011 was judged to be Hong Kong, measured at 89.7, while at the opposite end of the scale North Korea scores just a 1.

When the index was first published in 1995, at the tail end of the Thatcher and Major reforms, Britain was measured at an impressive 77.9. By contrast, the US scored 76.7 while Canada was the third of the three at 69.4.

Over the next 15 years, matters would change. While Gordon Brown added taxes and regulation to the British economy, Chrétien, Martin, and later Stephen Harper, continued to reform the Canadian economy. By 2011, the ordering of the three countries had flipped. Heritage judged Canada to be 80.8, the US 77.8 and the UK just 74.5.[92] Other rankings, such as the Cato Institute's Economic Freedom of the World, tell a similar story.[93]

More impressionistically, other institutions in Canada remain strong. Canada enjoys strong infrastructure, and remains attractive to foreign businesses through its closeness to the US market. The health system combines universal coverage paid for by the Government with private provision of the actual services. The points-based immigration system has allowed Canada to continue to attract highly skilled workers. According to the international PISA studies, its pupils are tenth in the world for maths, eighth for science and sixth for reading. By contrast, the UK is 28th for maths, 16th for science and 25th for reading – a similar performance to the US.[94]

It would of course be wrong to pretend that Canada is perfect, or that no other country has relevant lessons for the UK. Canada still remains behind the United States in productivity and Australia in growth. The Asian tiger economies have other lessons to teach on education and reducing regulation.

It takes boldness to turn a country around. Canada did not get it right with its first attempt at fiscal austerity, under the government of Brian Mulroney. Eventually, however, it learned that to make a real difference it would have to cut spending early and sharply. Every department would have to share in the burden. The Government had to rethink what it did, rather than try to 'salami slice' each individual budget.

Britain now is in a worryingly uncompetitive position. In the 1990s, it seemed that Britain might have finally turned its back on its slow postwar decline. Its economy was once more admired.

That success is now in danger of seeming more a blip than a trend. A legacy of a bloated state, high taxes and excessive regulation threatens to take the drive out of the British economy.

In many ways, Britain faces a harder task than Canada. It does not enjoy Canada's resilient financial sector, or its bounty of commodity exports. The windfall of North Sea oil is starting to peter away. Britain's adjustment has to be made in the face of the worldwide downturn, rather than the benign economy of the 1990s. While Canada's neighbour, the United States, continued to boom, Britain's neighbour, the Eurozone, looks if anything to be in an even worse position than us.

Even so, the task will not get any easier by putting it off. If Britain is to get its spending back under control, it has hard choices to make. If we want a more prosperous tomorrow, we must save more today.

Moreover, the story of Canada does eliminate many of our excuses. Canada doesn't achieve superior results through some special Scandinavian or Asian culture that the UK could never emulate. It doesn't take advantage of the economies of scale of a population of hundreds of millions. It is a developed, mature country, and doesn't have the ability to take advantage of easier catch-up growth. Nobody is suggesting that Canada will only thrive in the future as part of a larger political unit, rather than as part of a free trade area. The idea that any Canadian would want to become an American is laughable; they are rightly happy and content to remain as independent Canadians.

At the beginning of this millennium, Canada chose to liberalise its economy, to pay down its debt and to raise the standards its education system. The UK made the opposite choice.

3 Revenge of the Geeks

International league tables show that British pupils are falling behind their peers in South Korea or China. We have to stop lowering the bar in our schools, choose more academic subjects, and work longer hours.

According to Education Secretary Michael Gove, German statistician Andreas Schleicher is 'the most important man in English education'. A profile for *The Atlantic* magazine was headlined 'the world's schoolmaster'. President Obama's Secretary of Education, Arne Duncan, is equally a fan.[1] As head of the OECD's Programme for International Student Assessment (PISA), Schleicher is in charge of the ultimate schools league table: ranking the education systems of the OECD's members.

Schleicher was born in Hamburg in 1964. While his father was a professor of education, Schleicher initially had little interest in the subject. Originally an indifferent student, it was only after he discovered his passion for the harder sciences that he went on to do well at school. He graduated with a degree in Physics from the University of Hamburg in 1988, and went on to study maths at Deakin University in Australia. It was only after attending a lecture by T. Neville Postlethwaite, an English education scientist in 1986, that Schleicher realised he might have an interest in his father's subject after all. While Schleicher's father believed that the human nature of education made it impossible to measure, Postlethwaite believed that it was only by comparing the statistics across countries that one could decide what worked and what didn't.[2] In 1988, Postlethwaite asked Schleicher to help him with the first international study on reading and writing.[3] By 1994, Schleicher had joined the OECD in Paris.

By the late 1980s the OECD had started to take the idea of comparing the performance of the world's schools systems seriously. In 1981, the administration of the new President Ronald Reagan ordered the creation of a National Commission on Excellence in

Education. The Commission's report, *A Nation at Risk*, released two years later, shocked America. It found that 23 million adults and 17 per cent of American minors were illiterate.[4] Scores on the country's SAT (Standard Assessment Tasks) tests had dropped throughout the 1960s and 1970s. To Reagan, this was more than just a shocking waste of human potential – it was a national security risk. In the words of the report, 'the educational foundations of our society are presently being eroded by a rising tide of mediocrity that threatens our very future as a Nation and a people'.[5] Earlier, while running for election, Reagan had called for eliminating the entire US Department for Education.[6] After the release of the report, he changed course: education reform was to become one of the top priorities for his administration. As part of the reform programme, his administration desired data on what worked well elsewhere – and the OECD seemed the best able to provide it.

Originally reluctant, the OECD eventually gave in to its largest donor, and by 1988 the International Indicators of Educational Systems (INES) project was established. By the late 1990s, the OECD realised that it was not enough to try to compare and analyse already existing data. Instead, it determined to launch its own international survey: PISA. Schleicher was placed in charge. Many countries had boasted to him that they had the best schools systems in the world.[7] PISA would give him the opportunity to work out who was right, and who was in for a nasty surprise.

So far, there have been four rounds of the PISA tests, repeating every three years. The first took place in 2000, and took in 32 countries. Today, over 70 countries and more than 500,000 pupils are involved.[8] In each country, 5,000 pupils aged between 15 and 16 are chosen, and tested on their mathematics, reading and science. Unlike other international tests, PISA is less interested in how well pupils have done at learning a curriculum, and more interested in their ability at solving problems and applying basic skills. Each pupil is given a two-hour exam, including both multiple choice and longer written answers. Data from across the world are collected, and scaled so that the average score across the OECD is 500 points, and the standard deviation 100 points. Around two-thirds of students score between 400 and 600 points.[9] A follow-up study of 30,000 students in Canada found that that PISA score proved a better predictor of whether they'd go to college than their grades.[10]

In December 2001, the first results were released. Top of the pack on the main competency studied, reading, was Finland, with a score of 546 points. Japan did best overall, scoring 522 at reading, 557 at mathematics and 550 at science. Britain scored reasonably well, with an average 528 points, putting it in seventh place. The US did badly, scoring just under the OECD average – but then America had known since *A Nation at Risk* that its education system was in trouble.

It was in Schleicher's native Germany that the real shock came.

Germany had always been proud of its education system and intellectual heritage. It saw itself as Das Land der Dichter und Denker – the land of poets and philosophers. In the early nineteenth century, in the wake of their defeat at the hands of Napoleon, the Prussians had set about creating a new type of schooling system. In 1808, Wilhelm von Humboldt, a friend to Goethe and Schiller and himself an important philosopher, became the Minister for Education. Under his stewardship, Prussia created a system of free, compulsory public education that would soon be copied by the United States and Japan. Moreover, by combining teaching and research at the University of Berlin, Humboldt helped create the model for the modern university.

Two centuries later, the Germans assumed that their education system still remained one of the world's best. Without a central examination system, there was little data to tell them otherwise – until, that is, Schleicher's numbers arrived.

In the 2000 test, Germany scored just 484 points in reading, 490 in maths and 487 in science. That put it comfortably under the OECD average of 500, in the bottom third of industrial nations. Just as bad, the inequality between the best and worst students was larger than in any other country studied. A later study by the Education Ministry found that 30 per cent of university students dropped out before completing their degree, compared to 19 per cent in Britain. While 35 per cent of Britons hold a university degree, just 16 per cent of Germans do, the same proportion as Turkey or Mexico.[11]

As a nation, the Germans were horrified. A poll for the Allensbach Institute found 60 per cent of Germans 'alarmed'.[12] The newspapers ran six-page special reports on PISA. Between 2001 and 2008, the German paper *Süddeutsche Zeitung* published 253 articles on PISA. (By contrast, the eight major papers in the US published just eight articles between them.)[13] One television channel even launched a quiz programme, *The PISA Show*.[14] The Education Ministry promised to work 'day and night' on reforms.

Over the next decade, the Germans set to work to raise their performance. Teams were sent out all over the world to learn from the best. For the core subjects, maths, science, German and foreign languages, strict national standards were introduced. In a nation where responsibility for education was devolved to the states this represented a radical departure. These national standards set out the rigorous content that every student is expected to study. Regular monitoring was introduced to ensure the standards were met.

Boosting the curriculum, however, wouldn't be enough – students were also expected to work for longer and study harder. The decision was made to extend the school day. At the time of the first PISA test, German students spent only 796 hours each year in primary school. The OECD average was 841 hours.[15] Whereas previously students only attended school in the morning, a remnant of the system's agrarian past, today students in many schools are expected to stay until 4pm or later.

Reform to an education system takes time, and there remains significant room for improvement in the German system. Nevertheless, the latest PISA tests show that the country is heading in the right direction. Germany's performance in reading went up from 484 points in 2000 to 497 points in 2009, in maths from 490 points to 513 points, and in science from 487 points to 520 points.[16] The largest reason for the improvement was better performance from less privileged pupils. Germany succeeded in climbing the world league tables.

Unfortunately, one reason for Germany's relative improvement is that other countries are doing worse. Since the first PISA test, performance in Spain, France, Austria and the UK has fallen.[17] As more countries enter into the PISA process, the UK slides down the league tables – despite massive increases in spending on education. (Spending in Germany remained relatively constant.) In 2000, the UK was eighth in the world for reading and writing, at 523 points. In 2009, it was just 25th, at 494.

As with any ambitious statistical undertaking, the data from the PISA studies are far from perfect. Nevertheless, as Andreas Schleicher put it, there is little doubt that while other countries improved, the UK 'stagnated at best'.[18]

Downshifting

For many students sipping coffee in the common room, clubbing or lazing around appeals more than poring over a test tube or doing complicated sums. In the US around 40 per cent of those who intend to major in science or engineering switch their major or fail to get a degree.[19] Why is this? Because students view the courses as being too hard.

Take Biyan Zhou, a 22-year-old student at Carnegie Mellon, one of the world's top institutions for engineering. Encouraged by her mother and academic advisor, Zhou originally intended to major in electrical and computer engineering, recognising the advantages this would give her in a competitive jobs market. However, spending seven days a week in the lab, while achieving lower grades in engineering compared to other classes, changed her mind. Instead she switched to a major in psychology and policy management, where the median average earnings for a graduate are $38,000 lower. Since switching Zhou has a string of As rather than the mix of Bs and Cs she used to achieve in her engineering classes.[20] Zhou is not alone in finding classes in the arts easier than those in the sciences; this has been a longer-term trend in the US with undergraduates achieving often lower grades in chemistry or maths courses than in English.[21] In the modern culture of instant gratification, students go for the easier option. Higher grades in other subjects combined with the grind of long hours in the lab or sweating over irrational numbers provide students with the incentive to switch.

In Britain, while many will know of medical students who switch to history, or the physicist who switched to English, the trend of switching to an easier degree is far less pronounced than in the US. This can partly be attributed to the specialised nature of UK degrees, which makes it harder for students to switch subjects. Someone with the right combination of A Levels for a chemistry degree is unlikely to have the mix for one in French. Instead, the switch takes place at 16 or before, when students choose their A Level options. A failure of market information, and a preference for subjects they view as being easier, leads to students opting not to take maths beyond 16.[22] The result is the UK having the lowest proportion of studying maths post-16 amongst developed countries.[23] Even those who decide to continue with maths post-16 struggle to stick with it, and around 30 per cent choose not to carry on with the subject at A2.[24]

Instead of hard choices, students apply for a degree in media or business, which will often allow for the study of easier A Levels.[25] As with US college courses, science A Levels are more harshly marked than those in media and sociology, the difference being up to a grade.[26] In a culture of equivalence, where all subjects are deemed equal, students make the seemingly rational choice of going for the easier option. But by not taking a maths A Level they may sacrifice an extra £136,000 in lifetime earnings.[27]

One report quantified that the taxpayer was wasting £40 million per year on 401 university 'non-courses'. Such courses included specialist make-up design at the University of Bedfordshire, fiction and culture at the university of Glamorgan, aromatherapy and therapeutic bodywork at the University of Greenwich and martial arts and adventure tourism at the University of Derby.[28] In 2003, this trend led Education Minister Margaret Hodge to criticise the proliferation of 'Micky Mouse' degrees. By contrast, students seem less keen on taking up real work experience. The UK has one of the lowest participation rates in work placement schemes in Europe.[29]

The declining pull of the hard sciences is not restricted to Anglo-Saxon nations. Though it is still a high achiever in the international league tables for high school maths and science, Japan is also suffering from the same malaise. Japanese students are now the least likely to want to take the tough subjects of any leading economy. Only 35 per cent of students say they plan to pursue a career in science or technology.[30]

In the meantime the country's public education system expresses most concern about 'cramming establishments', despite the fact that the so-called *juku* are now the bastions of academic standards. The Government, under the influence of the teaching unions and fixated on equality, refuses to recognise *juku*, even though one in five primary schoolers and almost all university-bound high schoolers attend them.[31] As an institution the *juku* are very old, but they really took off in the 1970s. There are now 50,000 *juku* in Japan. So successful have *juku* been that they are being exported to China and other Asian economies, where they are popular with ambitious parents who want to give their child the edge.[32]

In South Korea, 'hypereducation' has gone even further. The exams which young Koreans take are crucial for determining which university they attend. In turn, their university determines the likely job-for-life corporate or government career they will commence afterwards. Competition is fierce, children are hungry to learn and succeed; parents are desperate for their child to advance. It is no surprise that the Koreans study so hard at school, or that their education system regularly ranks near the top of the international PISA rankings. Many students go straight from long days at school to studying all evening and weekend. In Seoul, as much as 16 per cent of a family's income is spent on private tuition on top of the state education system.[33] So popular are the *hagwon*, the Korean equivalent of *juku*, that some local authorities have tried to set limits on the hours the *hagwon* can study for. Freelance *hagparazzi* are paid to catch on hidden cameras any *hagwon* that try to break curfew.

Two Cultures

While students in developed countries are deserting the sciences, youngsters in India and Mexico are queuing up to enrol on these courses, believing that there will be a pot of gold awaiting them. High value services, such as research and programming, are increasingly a global market, with Indian graduates able to compete against those in the UK and the US in their delivery.[34] If you are in the top few per cent the world is open to you. You can earn hundreds of thousands as a 'quant' or programmer, the new 'Master of the Universe'. That market attracts countries 'on the way up'. When Berkeley offered its first Masters in Financial Engineering course, nearly a quarter of the students came from China.[35] The absolute brightest in Britain and the US can and do compete in the international geek contest.

Yet a British student who is middling-to-good is presented with very different choices. The domestic jobs market in Britain often values all degrees equally (or at least ones from the same institution). While over three-quarters of graduate jobs demand a 2.1, only a third of graduate jobs require a specific degree subject.[36] The Government itself is blasé about how hard a subject is. Its prestigious and highly competitive Fast Stream programmes, which recruit the future top civil servants, require a 2.1 regardless of institution or course.[37] The evidence suggests that the civil service lacks those people with a quantitative mindset. Take Trevor Wolley, Finance Director of the MOD who, when questioned about the overspend on various helicopter and equipment projects, admitted he didn't have a single financial qualification.

But why would a student put themselves through the hard graft when the jobs are open to those who have managed to spend their university days in the pub as well as the library? As a student you would have to be a bit crazy to attempt to do a harder subject and risk missing out on the 2.1. The result is that our employment market is not an accurate reflection of the real demand for skills in the global economy. Distinctions about capability and ability are much more obvious when maths and science are under discussion than when arts subjects are being considered. This makes arts subjects inherently attractive for the wavering student.

While many an Oxford classicist still enters the City in London, banks fill the need for mathematical knowledge with foreign quant experts. One banker estimated that only one in eight high-level mathematicians recruited in the City came from the UK.[38] This is hardly surprising given that in India and China top executives and bankers are often paid a lot less for doing the same job. The Chief Executive of the ICBC, by market capitalisation the world's largest bank, based in Hong Kong, earns $235,000 a year while the heads of the Bank of China and CCB earn $229,000 apiece.[39] Demand for top French maths graduates remains high, and recruiters openly admit that they only consider Oxbridge in the UK, compared to broader recruitment from France, Germany and Singapore.[40]

Although science is particularly affected, there is a wider problem with academic attainment overall. Large swathes of British culture takes a dim view of academic achievement. Take the case of *X Factor* contestant Ashley John-Baptiste. He was taken into care at the age of four. He was then fostered before spending two years in a children's home and attending three different primary schools. John-Baptiste then went to a comprehensive school in South London which had a high number of students who came from deprived backgrounds. By any measure his life to the age of 18 was a recipe for academic failure; except in his case it wasn't. Through sheer hard work he secured a place to read history at Cambridge before appearing on the *X Factor* as part of boy-band. The Risk. In a show which revels in telling contestant's life stories, John-Baptiste's was sure to be a highlight. Yet, while producers chose to emphasise how one contestant was abandoned by her mother and another spent time living in a squalid bedsit in a rough part of London, John-Baptiste's academic achievement was ignored.[41]

If academic prowess is distrusted generally in Britain, it is scientists who have been treated as a particular oddity. C.P. Snow famously took on the division between science and the arts in 'The Two Cultures' in 1956 arguing against the snobbery in British society that led Classics to be favoured over calculus. The response from F.R. Leavis, perhaps the paradigm of the 'literary intellectuals' he criticised, was mockery. Leavis simply dismissed Snow as a 'public relations man' for the scientific establishment. Increasingly, however, Snow's view of the importance of scientific literacy and culture has been picked up by policy-makers on both side of the Atlantic. American Presidents from Bush to Obama have indulged in periods of soul-searching, arguing that schools and colleges should train up more scientists and mathematicians.[42] Angela Merkel, a physicist from East Germany, is an exception in her scientific educational background. Eight out of nine of the top political positions in China are held by engineers. In India, it is normal for the Prime Minister to address the country's Science Congress – something which is not common in the West.[43]

In spite of the chill economic winds turning attention onto competitiveness, there remains a bias against subjects that can offer the highest wage. Today, the most popular career aspirations of pre-teens in the UK appear to be a sportsman, pop star or actor. Over half aspire to be famous over establishing a career.[44] Yet a generation ago, being a pop star or an actor didn't even make the top ten. Being a teacher or banker came top.[45] Indeed, despite the majority of pre-teens having a positive view of science, very few – less than a fifth – would consider it as a career option.[46] And whilst parents are more realistic than their children, their preference is for the professions, not the lab, with lawyer and medic coming out top.[47]

Unlike those from the backstreets of Bangalore, low-income students in Britain do not see study as a way out of poverty. This is bad news for those from the poorest backgrounds. If they take them at all, they often take A Levels that rule them out of science and maths at university. Students at comprehensive schools are seven times more likely to take media studies but only half as likely to take maths or physics compared to their privately educated peers.[48]

Only the LSE have revealed their real views, declaring a list of 'non-preferred subjects' like Law A Level, which will get you no nearer to a Court of Law than studying car mechanics. Nevertheless, the rise of the non-subject has been spectacular. Psychology is fast catching up with mathematics A Level in popularity in Britain's state schools. This is a subject for which there is very little genuine demand in the workplace.

Even if those at Eton and Harrow are more likely to have taken maths and the sciences at A Level, they tend to shy away from these subjects later on. Few from affluent backgrounds in the UK take science or, God forbid, maths at university. Instead they are more likely to study history, languages and classics.[49] Indeed, it seems the only section of society where there is a high uptake of science is male, ethnic minority students. Discounting all other factors, a top male student from an ethnic minority is more likely to read engineering or maths than an equally high achiever who happens to be white.[50]

At the top it remains acceptable not to understand science. The spirit of *Yes Minister*, where everyone in the room can discuss the Greek Aorist but are clueless about chemistry, is still strong in British boardrooms. In the recent financial crisis, problems were caused by owners not understanding managers and managers not understanding the rocket scientists working for them. The film *Margin Call* portrays the chaos in an investment bank where a mistake in an equation threatens to wipe out the firm's market capitalisation. When the analysts try to bring the impending disaster to the attention of the banks CEO, his response is one of incomprehension. 'Speak to me in plain English or as you would to a young child or golden retriever. It wasn't brains that got me here', he tells his subordinates.

The City's cult of the 'quant', who might have a PhD in theoretical physics or mathematical logic, created a division between the analysts and the managers. Quite simply, those in charge didn't understand the maths. The epitome of this cult was David Li. A brilliant Chinese mathematician with a PhD in statistics, his development of a Gaussian copula function for CDSs (credit default swaps) and CDOs (collateralised debt obligations) was lauded as a watershed in measuring risk.[51] Adopted by Standard & Poor's and Moody's, his formula became widely accepted in measuring risk. It even formed part of the Basel II regulations.[52] The problem was, as Li himself admitted in 2005, that few people understood how the model worked.[53] Rather than questioning the outputs, fund managers did exactly what Li warned them not to do. They treated the model as a magic box believing everything that came out of it.[54] The result was a recipe for disaster. Fund managers who made the calls didn't understand the maths, while the quants failed to point out any weaknesses.[55] As the market in CDOs collapsed in 2008, the weakness of the model was increasingly clear; blind faith in the maths effectively 'felled Wall Street'.[56] The divide between the two cultures has serious consequences.

Geek Chic

A strong ability in quantitative methods is viewed as being akin to membership of an outlandish cult. Papers occasionally run headlines like 'Why geeks are suddenly chic',[57] yet the business ends of science and maths remain deeply niche. While Leslie Simon's book *Girl Geeks Unite* may have the subtitle 'How Fangirls, Bookworms, Indie Chicks, and Other Misfits Are Taking Over the World', it outlines a diverse range of groups. Rather than being viewed as part of the everyday mainstream, each type of geek is viewed as a separate clan with identifiable characteristics. In a world of increasingly targeted advertising, the mainstream media have latched onto the value of targeting individual groups. Broadcaster CNN even has a website hosting a 'Geek Out!' blog that describes itself as featuring 'stories from a nerd's perspective that you can still share with your "normal" friends and family'.[58] While the burgeoning number of websites and books devoted to 'geek culture' might serve as a way to share experience with fellow geeks, they do little to increase the mainstream popularity of studying science. Senior Google Executive Marissa Mayer has blamed the 'geek culture' as one of the reasons why so few women go into tech careers.[59] While the idea that a career in tech is nerdy deters both men and women, it has a stronger impact on women who view these careers as being divorced from everyday life.[60] And, though there are short-term boosts in popularity when a new film comes out like *The Social Network*, nothing has broken the glamour of arts subjects for aspiring students.

In fact, it turns out that if you're female, majoring in mathematics and science can even damage your sex life. Women feel less attractive to men if they have been thinking about sums.[61] The fear of maths damaging your sex life is not just restricted to women. A typical post in a student chatroom is titled 'Would majoring in economics/ mathematics make me undesired in the dating scene?' A student asks if he 'would be considered as unattractive if I have a major that is Math or linked with Math' and whether he 'should continue with this path or change'.[62] With the perception that maths and science are only for the brainiacs, there is a fear that pursuing a career in it dooms you to unpopularity.

The proportion of women studying tech subjects in the UK and US has plummeted, particularly in new fields like computer science where there are some of the best opportunities. And while both countries have witnessed a steep decline, women form a smaller proportion of tech graduates and workers in the UK than in the US.[63] But those women who are prepared to put up with the apparent ignominy of working in tech are set to benefit. Pay is not only higher in tech careers, the pay gap between genders is also smaller. While women in the US earn on average 21 per cent less than their male peers, for those in tech careers the gap shrinks to 14 per cent.[64]

The definition of success in the US and the UK couldn't be more different from emerging markets. In contrast to Britain's fame obsession, success in India is becoming a mid-trained computer engineer or technician.[65] If you want to make your taxi driver sit up in Bangalore, don't say you're going to the Big Brother house, say you're going to Electronics City to see Narayana Murthy, the billionaire founder of Infosys.[66]

These jobs are inherently meritocratic, compared with fields like media or journalism which rely on contacts. As serial tech entrepreneur Audrey MacLean puts it, 'either you have the goods or you don't'.[67] Meritocracy is a big consideration in a country like India where nearly a quarter of politicians have been served with a criminal charge and nepotism is rife.[68] When three-quarters of the population live on less than $2 a day, a starting salary of up to $6,000, and an industry average of $20,000 for a software developer, is a strong incentive to study hard.[69] The result is that competition is fierce, with 61 students vying for every available place at the country's elite and highly selective Indian Institutes of Technology. This is far above the average of just over five applicants per place at Oxford.[70]

In India the International Physics Olympiad receives the same amount of media as the Olympics. The Indians see brainpower as a sport in which they can excel. Rather than covering the latest royal to tumble out of Boujis, the Indian press celebrates the highest performer in the entrance exams for the ultra-elite Indian Institutes of Technology.[71] The year's topper, as they're widely known, receives widespread media coverage, their success splashed across the front pages of national newspapers and interviewed for India's version of CNN about their experiences.[72]

Nitin Jain grew up in a suburb of Faridabad just outside New Delhi where, like many teenage boys, he enjoyed playing computer games such as 'Grand Theft Auto' or table tennis with his friends. But he was also the 2009 topper and a three-time medallist in the International Science Olympiads. After his success in the entrance exams he was thrust into the public eye. A party by his parents to celebrate his results attracted such widespread media coverage that he is recognised by strangers in the street – a fate normally reserved for celebrities in the UK.[73] And though described as shy by journalists, Jain has made a sensation of it. In 2010 he published a popular guide to success in the entrance exams to the Institutes of Technology, even though in his own words his method is a simple one: 'hard work'.[74] Fans can even find out his secrets on his website, while his name is such a recognisable brand that his family took action in the Delhi High Court to stop commercial coaching institutes using it.[75]

When women in emerging economics are kept out of tech careers it is for entirely different reasons – it's about power and the perception that careers in science and technology are more suited to men than women.[76] No doubt this is partly because, with lower rates of female literacy, women are less likely than men to take a degree.[77] Yet around the developing world this view of tech careers being more suited to men is starting to change. In Mexico, students are now more likely than those in the UK to reject such a view.[78] Indeed, unlike their Western counterparts, emerging economies have seen the share of women studying computer science and engineering increase drastically. India has witnessed the proportion of female IT undergraduates double, while engineering is the second biggest growth area for female students.[79] In Malaysia tech jobs are dominated by women who see it as a 'clean career'. It's also about national pride. Indians and Mexicans are far more likely to believe that it is very important for their country to lead the world in science compared to those in the US, the UK and Japan.[80] The excitement of scientific advance exemplified by the Space Programme seems to have left the West and headed elsewhere.

India has many hundreds of thousands of scientists, engineers, technicians and mathematicians, with large numbers of qualified technicians and a small number who go on to elite level. While the Indian Institutes of Technology recruit 7,500 students a year, about the same as go to Oxbridge, the country as a whole produces nearly half a million engineering graduates a year.[81] These numbers are set to explode. Currently only 12 per cent of young Indians go on to university but the Government has set a target of 30 per cent by 2025 – in line with many countries in the West.[82] The students at the Indian Institutes of Technology have doubled in numbers in the last few years.[83] India does of course have its problems. You are unlikely to catch cholera in Britain or experience the grinding poverty that is a fact of everyday life for many in India. When it comes to high levels of education, it is still a comparatively small elite who gain the rewards. While graduate numbers dwarf those in the UK, they only represent a small proportion of the population. As only 40 per cent of young people attend secondary school, large swathes of the population, often the poorest in society, lack the opportunity to get ahead.[84] Yet in spite of all these deficiencies, India's economy will grow consistently in the coming years.[85]

Building the Pyramid

There are 2.4 million people working in the UK with a science of tech degree. That is a larger proportion of the working-age population than in the US, Germany or Japan.[86] Yet the strong results are not translating into a mass movement. There is a column of talent rather than a pyramid. The top performers are a large proportion of the total number of students. For example, last year just over 75,000 students took an A Level in maths, broadly the same as the total number of undergraduates in maths and the physical sciences.[87] If this strength was used to its full potential, the country would be able to fulfil all its requirements with thousands of engineers and computer experts. What's missing is a working knowledge of these subjects for those who qualify in other areas – or who may switch to other subjects later on, or those who become mid-level professionals. Economics lecturers tear their hair out at the poor mathematics knowledge of students. The cycle perpetuates in the next generation when ranks of primary school teachers, journalists and politicians are barely numerate.

Sometimes there is no choice at all for the keen student. Only half of sixth forms at comprehensive schools offer further maths, excluding a significant proportion of the population going for a degree that will take them into the international rocket scientist league.[88] And while the numbers taking A Levels in physics and maths have recovered in the last few years, much of this is making up for the steep decline in numbers (by up to a third) of the preceding decade.[89] This lack of people with mid-level qualifications in science and technology is a drag on the economy.

Emerging countries are rapidly catching up with West when it comes to scientific development. The most successful will be those which can absorb and modify ideas from all over the world in their domestic economy.[90] In Germany and Switzerland, high-tech car plants have the workers with the requisite skill to develop models.[91] In the UK an insufficient quantity of innovators who understand technology, maths or science in Britain has stunted efforts to develop or to 'leap forward'. The intellectual capital created is often absorbed by those countries that have a broader skills base and are able to innovate in their factories and labs. Yet Britain has historically been slow in taking advantage of these opportunities. Alfred Marshall's observation that 'the small band of British scientific men have made revolutionary discoveries in science; but yet the chief fruits of their work have been reaped by businesses in Germany and other countries where industry and science have been in close touch with one another' remains as true today as it was when he made it in 1919.[92] Britain still hasn't learned from past mistakes.

Thus top-performing UK universities that head the world's charts for research are like the academic Premier League: they rely on foreign players. The world ranking table of universities lists 29 UK universities in the top 200, compared to Germany with 14 and France with three, just above Spain's two and Italy's zero.[93] Britain has two vital strengths; speaking English and the openness of the academic job market. European countries, where the tradition is to appoint locals, often do not have the same calibre of people in their research institutions.[94] Yet if Britain is to remain a major player in the academic leagues it needs to turn out the next generation of Nobel Prize winners. Over half of all postgraduate students studying mechanical engineering in the UK are from overseas, a situation repeated in many other scientific fields.[95] Even if there isn't any indigenous talent, wealthy Western countries have often been able to attract the brightest and the best from overseas. In the last decade the majority of appointees to UK university positions in mathematics were educated overseas.[96] Yet as emerging economies fill up their own demand for highly skilled workers, this is much less likely to occur. Just over a decade ago the majority of graduates from India's elite Indian Institutes of Technology moved overseas for further study. Today, most go into the country's booming economy.[97] Governments in both India and China have active policies to make it easier and more attractive for citizens abroad to return home.[98]

National debates about 'making things' miss the point. Manufacturing is likely to continue in Britain. The price of oil and increased automation may result in more goods being produced close to source.[99] The question is where the intellectual capital will lie. Already low-tech manufacturing only accounts for 14 per cent of all manufactured exports with high-tech manufacturing forming a greater proportion in the UK than in either Germany or France.[100] Technology is driving an hourglass economy and the growth of two types of jobs that will dominate the future job market – high-skilled professionals and lower-skilled personal services. Over the last 15 years the numbers of highly-paid technical and professional jobs have increased by a third, while middle-income jobs have been squeezed out – dropping by 13 per cent.[101]

The future economic battle will not be about national champions fighting each for world domination. It will be about which nation can make the strongest intellectual and practical contribution to global enterprise. In a globalised world, international networks are essential for science. There is greater international collaboration on ideas than ever before; since the mid 1990s there has been a sharp increase in the number of UK research papers with a foreign co-author.[102] In recent years the largest growth centres for scientific research are not London, Tokyo and New York, but rather Shanghai, Nanjing and Sao Paulo. If a country tries to build stand-alone 'assets' – whether they are companies or institutions – this will fail. The countries with the highest quotient of innovators who are able to tap into and extract from international network will succeed. Forward-looking countries recognise this. The Vietnamese Government has a policy of 'actively expanding co-operation and international integration in science and technology'.[103] And while US patent registrations from China remain small compared to Japan, the UK and Germany, they are rapidly growing – in 1999 China registered only 90 patents, but by 2009 the figure had increased to 1,655.[104] Anyone, anywhere, can access the latest ideas and modify them for their market.

Lowering the Bar

Low-wage workers from the US to Germany to the UK are seeing very little improvement in their salaries. Take Eric Saragoza, who previously worked at the iPod factory in Silicon Valley as an engineer. His job is now done by an army of cheaper and faster engineers in the massive iPod plant in China. He now works at an electronics temp agency. For $10 an hour with no benefits, he wipes thousands of glass screens and tests audio ports by plugging in headphones.[105] These changes in circumstances are often blamed on globalisation. It is true that cheaper and more qualified workers around the globe have forced faster progress. However, underlying this shift is the relentless advance of technology and the eventual replacement of basic skilled jobs with machines.

To get ahead in the new type of jobs you need to be able to reason and think logically. Countries' long-term growth is inalterably linked to the skills of their workforce. So how do countries enhance them? The answer is partly through the study of the key tech subjects of engineering, maths and computer sciences.[106] And quality out-performs quantity almost every time, when it comes to maximising impact. Five years of high-quality maths education will trump seven low-grade ones.[107]

While improving these skills helps growth, they can't be restricted to the few. The biggest effect happens when on top of a large number of people with high-level skills almost everyone has the basic and mid-level skills.[108] On the latter measure Britain needs radical measures.

As a trading economy, Britain is particularly in need of this dual performance. The more open the economy the more important the ability to reason for growth.[109] With Britain open to international trade, top quality education will provide a much bigger boost than in closed off Cuba.[110] As India, Mexico and China become more open, improving these skills and abilities will have an increasingly positive effect on their economies, speeding up their technological progress.[111]

Professions like law and medicine are becoming more technical in scope. In the insurance industry, extensive medical data, demographics and customer profiling are now available to generate more sophisticated calculations of risk. If James Bond were a spy today he wouldn't be looking for a secret nuclear bunker in a volcano – he would be conducting high-level industrial espionage. The growth of digital technology has sparked a boom in areas like intellectual property law. Global trade in IP licences alone is worth more than £600 billion a year – 5 per cent of world trade and rising. UK firms now spend more on intangible investment, or investment in IP, than fixed assets. Service jobs in law and consulting increasingly need people with advanced maths and science degrees who understand complex patents and trademarks. And the technology revolution is far from running out of steam, as two-thirds of the world is yet to be directly connected to the internet.[112]

Our obsession with smart phones has created a multi-million pound industry in Facebook and phone apps. As an industry which has a value of half a billion pounds a year, the 'app economy' demonstrates the integral role that technology plays in the modern market.[113] Sixty per cent of teenage smartphone users admit to being highly addicted. All these new sectors are set to increase exponentially in the coming years.[114] The creation of apps is something the UK currently excels in with the creators of TweetDeck, Last.fm and Moo.com – the creators of the ubiquitous Moshi Monsters – all based in Shoreditch's Silicon Roundabout.[115] However, it is only through a technically literate and highly educated workforce that the UK, and the rest of the West, will be able to continue to take advantage of these opportunities. Otherwise jobs in these emerging sectors will be snapped up by highly educated, tech savvy and low-cost workers in Bangalore and Guadalajara.

While the figures are stark, few are prepared to take the hard medicine. Many parents are unwilling to fund extra study. In Mexico half of all students take additional maths classes after school but in the UK that figure drops to less than a third.[116] Meanwhile, in Japan, over three-quarters of students attend additional maths classes, while in South Korea many families spend a tenth of their income on private tuition.[117] While parents would rather their children were scientists and engineers than lawyers or business executives, they aren't so keen on their children being mathematicians.[118] And numbers studying science courses remain stubbornly constant as demand for media studies increases exponentially in Britain.[119]

Decades of efforts have been put into making science and maths fun, exciting and relevant. A website launched by the last government to promote science and maths at A Level pointed to jobs in cosmetics and media, promising things like 'in the cosmetics industry you get loads of free beauty products'. It assured aspiring students that 'scientists are sometimes asked to take part in TV, radio and magazine interviews'.[120] A head at a Further Education college said that students have to be tricked into taking hard subjects. He believed that colleges have to fool kids into thinking they are studying media studies or car mechanics to get them to take an interest in programming or software engineering. The apogee of this trend can be witnessed in a visit to the Science Museum, where the focus is too often on gizmos and gadgets with 'interactivity' as the watchword. The National Gallery is lauded for its exhibition of da Vinci's paintings and Tate Modern offers up challenging new art. The Science Museum, however, appears to need to ensure its exhibitions are relevant and help make science available – not do the hard stuff.

In primary schools, the trend has been about understanding using tortured methods like 'chunking' and 'horizontal addition', rather than practising the difficult sums that lead to long-term fluency. Copious materials have been produced explaining to parents why they can't do their children's homework. The BBC printed an article on its site in 2010 entitled 'Why parents can't do the maths today'. It explained that 'Long division and long multiplication have been replaced in schools by chunking and gridding. While the new methods are meant to make maths easier, parents have been left scratching their heads.'[121] Indeed, education experts in other countries have been left scratching their heads as to why the entire British education system has adopted an untried method for teaching maths, which only fails to bring students up to standards that compare with top performers in the world.

In short, Britain has tried to change maths and science to fit the wider cultural mores of the age. It has not adapted to deal with the new global social and economic reality. It's akin to turning up to the Olympics with a set of hurdles designed to suit the British physique rather than training athletes to take on competitors. This approach is doomed to fail.

The bald fact is that the only successful approach to poor performance has turned out to be hard work. Attempts to make subjects more relevant often just enforce bad attitudes. Students in the UK and the US spend less time in the classroom between the ages of 11 and 18 doing maths and science than their Indian counterparts. No wonder Indians have the experience to tough out a university course in the subject. It is not only students who are unwilling to work hard. The average Singaporean works two hours and twenty minutes a day longer than the average Brit.[122]

A 2007 study by the Higher Education Policy Institute found that the average student at a UK university worked 26 hours per work – with students at the Russell Group of top universities studying 28 hours per work, and the rest around 24 hours per week.[123] These averages mask wide differences. An average student studying Physics at Cambridge works 45 hours per week, compared to a student at Brighton University who spends 15 hours per week on Social Studies. The better universities do not just benefit from selecting the brightest students – they work them much harder too.

The same study found that, overall, students in the UK work less hard than at other comparable European universities – and around seven hours per week less than the European average. What mattered most was setting high expectations.[124] Meanwhile, workers in the UK are less productive per hour worked than in the US, Germany or France.[125]

Bottom of the Class

Despite being 28th in the 2009 OECD PISA tables for mathematics and 16th for science, few in the UK seem to be shocked. The PISA shock that so impacted Germany has yet to arrive in Britain.

Instead, attracted by the idea of longer lie-ins for future generations, some in Britain want their children to sit back and enjoy the fruits of their prosperity. Emma Duncan, the deputy editor of *The Economist*, said: 'I'll trade a few places on the global league table for those benefits.'[126] Yet are we being kind to be cruel. Too much pandering early on in a child's life and a student's academic career may not produce the resilience to compete later on. Apprentices in engineering now complain that the trigonometry they have learned at school is too weak for what is expected by employers. Failure to address this problem may mean generations here remain in the slow lane. They have no desire for this. Too many are willing to let Britain slip gently into obscurity.

But not all Britons are prepared to throw in the towel before the real race has started. Internationally, Britain's elite is still able to succeed, as is demonstrated by top British executives leading companies the world over. Take, for example, Sir Howard Stringer, the current head of Sony; or Sir George Buckley, the head of the US conglomerate 3M.[127] Not only do the best British executives have the advantage of speaking the international language of business, but they are respected for their cultural flexibility and high-level skills, which often gives them the edge over their American and European competitors. In particular, British petroleum and mining executives are in huge demand internationally despite coming from a small talent pool. This is driven to a large extent by the know-how they develop at leading British universities, such as Imperial College, which offer well respected and highly rigorous postgraduate courses in petroleum engineering.[128]

Britain's top universities are still amongst the greatest in the world. Despite having only 3 per cent of the world's researchers, Britain turns out 6 per cent of the world's academic articles and 11 per cent of citations; more articles and citations per researcher than the US, China, Japan and Germany.[129] And students from around the world want to study at UK universities, the brand recognition of which is only matched by members of the US Ivy League. Despite increased competition from universities in their homeland, students from countries as diverse as India, Malaysia and Nigeria still want to study in Britain. Since 2004, the number of Indian students at UK universities has increased two-and-half-fold.[130] To cope with this demand, British universities are increasingly offering UK-validated courses that can be wholly studied overseas. The appetite, especially from Asia's aspirant middle classes, is great. The numbers have increased by a quarter in the last year alone.[131]

British Chinese youngsters are not just the highest performing ethnic group in England at GCSE level – their success cuts across class and income. Chinese students on free school meals out-perform the national average of all students, rich and poor. In 2009, 71 per cent of

Chinese children on free school meals won five good GCSEs (including English and Maths) – Chinese children not on free school meals only did 1 per cent better. Similar results have been recorded at primary school level in English Key Stage 2 scores. What appears to make these students stand out is parental aspiration, coupled with discipline, which – irrespective of class or parental occupation – translates into extra homework, tuition or classes outside school hours.

Nat Wei, a social entrepreneur from a Chinese background, is the youngest Member of the House of Lords. He grew up in humble surroundings in Tooting, where he attended state schools. He commented on the drug use prevalent at his school and on how he was bullied for taking his studies seriously. Nat went on to read Modern Languages at the University of Oxford, before working in senior positions in Teachfirst and ARK, organisations involved in improving education provision in the UK.

It is very interesting that at his school, taking studies seriously was seen as a bullyable offence by his peers. Even stranger is the fact that when you ask young people why they admire the celebrities of choice they aspire to be like, their wealth always comes out very highly. It is therefore the case that we need to help our young people to see the link between success and earning potential.

Ofsted's new chief inspector, Sir Michael Wilshaw, has also signalled a cultural shift in teaching, drawing from his experience as head teacher of Mossbourne Academy in Hackney. At Mossbourne, he pioneered a culture in which background would never be allowed as an excuse for failure. If students started to fall behind, they would be kept for longer at the end of the school day to help them catch up.[132] In his new role, Sir Michael has warned coasting schools they will have to do better to maintain their current rankings.

The signs are there that, as a whole, the younger generation doesn't accept the defeatist narrative of their elders and that students in Britain are beginning to 'get this'. Not brought up in the cosy European tent, they are realising that to get ahead they need to study the right subjects. In particular, students are starting to recognise the importance of maths. The last year alone witnessed an 8 per cent increase in the subject at A Level, and since the subject's nadir in 2005 the numbers taking it have increased by 57 per cent. The same is true at university where the rise in the number of applicants to read science and tech subjects has outstripped the general increase in applicants.[133] The introduction of higher tuition fees means there is a greater incentive for students to take degrees which offer a higher financial return. The result is that, while applications for the Arts and Social Sciences have seen sharp decreases, mathematics and the sciences have held up.[134] A similar phenomenon has been taking place in the US where, since 2010, there has been an uptick in the number of computer science majors, reversing the recent downward trend. Stanford, in particular, has seen numbers double since 2008. And not all are spreading doom and gloom: Mehran Sahami, associate chairman for computer science education at Stanford, believes this could be a turning point for computer science, with students inspired by the success of firms like Facebook, Google and Apple.[135]

But is Britain getting it fast enough? The political battle going on at the moment is between those who want open competition with the world and those who want Britain to slope off into the twilight. There is no need for a managed decline, but Britain will only get there if people are willing to take the tougher options.

4 Work Ethic

Once they enter the workplace, the British are among the worst idlers in the world. We work among the lowest hours, we retire early and our productivity is poor. Whereas Indian children aspire to be doctors or businessmen, the British are more interested in football and pop music.

Grafters, first and foremost. When the Royal Society for the Encouragement of Arts (RSA) conducted in-depth interviews with taxi drivers across the UK, the common trait that stands out amongst a diverse group – a self-styled 'odd bunch' – is work ethic.[1] 'If you drive a taxi you have to be very, very patient; nice people, bad people, traffic, accidents, everything – you have to be very patient.' The RSA found that taxi drivers admire people that 'make their own luck'. Pioneers like Lord Sugar, Margaret Thatcher and Rudi Giuliani are singled out. Strongly meritocratic, one driver waxes:

> You've probably guessed, I'm not a great socialist … I believe in a work ethic … not a great one for the Nanny State. I think where we've got to in helping people is over the top. I know people who play the system.

The sharpest criticism is reserved for the lazy, feckless, benefits cheats, 'talentless' celebrities and those who live beyond their means on credit. Don't get them started on public sector pensions.

The cabbies' motivation is straightforward: 'Work hard, play hard – and by playing I mean buying the cars I want, spending money on the kids, getting them the things that they want.' But the code of the cabbie is not just about making money. A professional and patriotic sense of pride motivates the drivers: 'The taxi is valeted twice a week. I get the exterior done at the car wash, and then I do the interior myself. And my brother does the same. It might have to do with OCD!' Personal pride extends to Queen, country and city, and not just in the capital. 'I like to make sure my passengers have a comfortable ride so they use me and my firm again and have a good impression of Birmingham', says one.

Stung by high fuel prices, the drivers are sceptical about the price they will have to pay to 'green' the British economy:

> We're taxed massively for this climate change, [while] you've got China laughing all the way to the bank with 6 per cent growth and the biggest economy of the world. We're doing our bit and I'd like to see everybody do their bit.

Nobody understands their ethos and aspirations better than John Griffin, the founder of Addison Lee minicabs, now a multi-millionaire.

Griffin has been called Britain's most successful taxi driver.[2] As a child, Griffin had been forced to leave school after contracting TB from a pail of milk on a school trip.[3] Despite starting his working life with no qualifications, he managed to obtain a position with an accountancy firm. More bad luck occurred when his father's roads and sewer company ran into trouble. Griffin quit his accountancy job to help out, taking a minicab job on the side to make ends meet. Deciding that he could run a minicab firm better than the management companies he worked for, in 1975 he set out in business on his own. Every morning he would leave his Potters Bar home at 6am and not return until 8pm that night.[4] To advertise his new venture, he printed out 100,000 business cards, and delivered them door to door.[5]

The company now runs over 4,000 cars, making an average 25,000 journeys a day. Addison Lee is the biggest buyer of Ford Galaxies in the world.[6] More than 50 per cent of the FTSE 100 companies use Addison Lee minicabs.[7] Griffin's philosophy is that working hard and treating his staff and customers right is the way to success. He argues that as long as you are prepared to take care of the customer, economic recession shouldn't stand in the way of business success.

Addison Lee's drivers work on a freelance basis. They can net £600 per week in take-home pay. But they have to work for it – around 60 hours per week.

The pay is similar to that of a tube train driver. Like the tube driver, the cabbie has to keep his carriage in a good condition – washing it, servicing the engine, and keeping the interior clean. But the real expertise lies in developing the notorious 'Knowledge' of their patch. In the capital, drivers need a detailed knowledge within a six-mile radius of Charing Cross. All-London drivers have to learn 320 routes. They also need to know all the landmarks and places of interest. This is no mean cerebral feat. Several neuroscientific studies have shown that studying for the test creates a noticeable difference in the size of the posterior hippocampus, the part of the brain dedicated to familiar spaces.[8]

Both the cabbie and the tube driver are put through the hoops before they can get into the driver's seat. For the tube driver, formal training lasts 22 weeks, with a further five to six weeks of 'on the job' training. In London, it takes minicab drivers twelve weeks to get a licence, whereas for a black-cab driver it takes two to three years to pass the All-London Knowledge necessary to drive around Greater London.

While the technical expertise may be analogous – and often underestimated – the contrast in financial rewards for hours worked is glaring. Both work in shifts, including irregular hours. But cabbies are effectively freelance, so they set their own hours. Still, working 60 hours per week, the Addison Lee cabbie still won't match what the tube driver takes home working an average of 35 hours per week. Thanks to tough bargaining by the unions, tube-driver pay is set to rise from £46,000 to over £50,000 – roughly double a nurse's pay.[9]

The tube driver also benefits from 29 days' paid holiday each year and a generous pension scheme, highly subsidised by the taxpayer, that allows him to retire at 60. The cabbie does not have these perks. If he doesn't work, he doesn't get paid. He is left to his own devices to graft to save enough for a summer holiday and retirement. The cabbie's ethos of self-reliance contrasts with the cosseted and heavily unionised world of the tube driver. Meanwhile, represented by militant RMT union boss Bob Crow, tube walkouts are regularly used to ramp up salary and other benefits. Tube drivers enjoy bonuses of up to £1,800 for working during the Olympics, and inflation-busting pay rises despite the pay freeze across the rest of the public sector.

This is just one snapshot of what is going on in modern Britain. The polarisation between those working very hard to make ends meet and those who enjoy public subsidies is apparent elsewhere. In 2008, a BBC documentary, 'The Poles are Coming' interviewed a range of employers and employees doing semi- or low-skilled work. Tomas, a Lithuanian stonemason near Peterborough, works from 7am to 5pm for £300 per week. His British manager extols the attitude of the migrant labour he employs:

They're never late; they're always enthusiastic. As soon as they've finished one job, if they can't find their own next job, which they normally do, they'll quickly come and ask what's wanted of them.[10]

Mariusz, a Polish migrant, gets to work for 6am. After a two-hour commute, he puts in ten hours each day fruit-picking. He earns £7 per hour and finds a couple of hours each day to work on his English, wryly noting: 'There are 24 hours in every day.' He doesn't feel guilty about stealing jobs from British workers because, as he laconically notes: 'There are no English people in this field.'

Outside the local JobCentre, the presenter of the documentary, Tim Samuels, talks to some UK-born jobseekers:

Samuels:	How desperate are you to get a job?
Interviewee 1:	Pretty desperate.
Samuels:	Would you fancy doing some vegetable picking tomorrow.
Interviewee 1:	Er ... no ...
Samuels:	There's loads of jobs that are needed to do in the farms: picking vegetables, packing them into boxes, getting £7 an hour minimum.
Interviewee 2:	Well that's where all the Poles and Czechs are, ain't it? Doing that sort of shit?
Samuels:	Why aren't you guys doing that sort of work?
Interviewee 2:	Because I don't want to work with a load of foreigners ...
Samuels:	But, they're doing the jobs that you want to do.
Interviewee 2:	[Opens a can of beer.]

In 2007, Sainsbury's caused some controversy when the company praised the 'superior' work ethic of migrant workers from Eastern Europe, and expressed the hope that it would rub off on 'domestic colleagues'.[11] Similarly, garden centre boss Richard Haddock complained that the school leavers allocated to him by the JobCentre were 'unsuited for the world of work'. Last year, Indian steel tycoon Ratan Tata complained in a similar way that clock-watching UK managers were unwilling 'to go the extra mile', and seemed never to be found in the office past 3.30pm on a Friday.[12]

So much for Britain's legendary Protestant work ethic. But how far can we generalise from anecdotal experience?

Idlers of the World?

Historically, continental Europeans led the way when it came to hard work. In 1870, average working hours in the Netherlands, Germany and France were over 3,000 per year, considerably more than the US, Australia or Britain.[13] Between the 1920s and 1970s, those countries converged on a downward trend. From the 1970s, they reversed position – by 2000, Americans, Australians and Britons were working between 1,700 and 1,900 hours per year, substantially more than their continental Europeans colleagues.

Figure 4.1 shows the international postwar trends in working hours from 1950 to 2009.[14] The overall number of hours worked has fallen across the board. However, Asian workers remain by far the hardest working, with Europeans – including the UK – steadily working less and less.

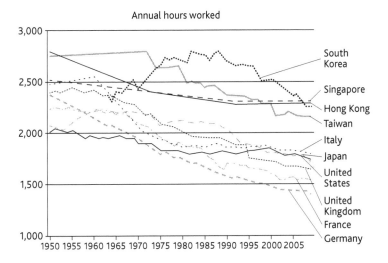

Figure 4.1

According to the Eurostat figures for 2011, the average working week in the UK is now broadly in line with the European average. At the same time, OECD figures show Western Europe – and the UK – trailing India, China, the US, Canada, Japan and Mexico.[15]

While Europeans have become less hard-working, Britain has become more European in its work habits. Historian Niall Ferguson puts it more bluntly: 'Europeans today are the idlers of the world.'[16] Ferguson believes that protracted education and longer retirement has led to a smaller proportion of Europeans actually being available for work. Of a smaller labour force, a larger proportion is unemployed – rising to 23 per cent in Spain.

Europeans in work are also more likely to go on strike. Sometimes strikes can shut down whole cities, making matters still worse. In 2010, French President Sarkozy tried to bring in austerity measures, including raising the retirement age from 60 to 62. The result was the worst strikes in France in 15 years. In Marseilles, 4,000 tonnes of rubbish were left on the streets, roads were blockaded, and ships proved unable to dock.[17]

When you include shorter working days and longer holidays, Europeans work much less hard than their American, let alone Asian, colleagues. Between 2000 and 2009, the average German worked 14 per cent fewer hours than the average Briton and 20 per cent fewer hours than the average American. The average American, in turn, worked at least 18 per cent less hours than the average worker from South Korea, Singapore or Hong Kong.[18]

Within the UK itself, the picture becomes more complicated. With 38 per cent of the population over 15 years old not working, Britain has a larger proportion of economically inactive people than the US, China or Singapore – but smaller than France or Germany.[19] Since 1993, Britain has seen significant increases in the number of full-time students, long-term sick, and retired.[20] But are those in work peddling harder, for longer, to make up for the large numbers out of work?

The bottom 10 per cent of full-time workers worked 32 hours a week in 2011. That is a fifth less than the 10 per cent working the longest hours (52 hours per week). However, since 1997 the bottom 10 per cent have actually increased their hours – by one per week – whilst the top 20 per cent have cut back on working time. The most diligent 10 per cent still work four hours per day more than the 10 per cent least diligent.

Once they enter the workplace, the British have long been less productive than workers in other Western countries. For each hour we work, we produce much less wealth. British workers are 11 per cent less productive than the average worker in the other G7 countries.

In 2010, the productivity gap between the UK and the US was wider than it has been since 1995. American workers are 35 per cent more efficient than the British.[21]

While Britain has suffered from low productivity for decades, over the course of the 1990s the UK seemed to finally begin catching up. Unfortunately, by the beginning of the millennium this growth had stalled. Between 1991 and 2004, the growth in UK productivity was larger than for any other G7 country. Between 2004 and 2010, it was slower than the average.[22] Even this temporary surge was largely a private sector phenomenon. Between 1997 and 2008, the ONS judges that the private sector became 20 per cent more efficient. At the same time, despite the large increases in spending, productivity in the public sector actually fell by 3.4 per cent.[23]

But does it matter that, as a nation, we are working less hard? As business leaders attest, it makes a big difference to business growth having employees willing to 'go the extra mile'. Generally, the more economic activity we engage in, the greater the national income. The importance of the work ethic becomes even more apparent when you include the public sector. The fewer people there are driving economic growth, the less tax revenue there will be to support those not in work –because they are studying, retired on a state pension or claiming income support.

Domestically, the declining British work ethic has important social implications too. Worklessness is a dangerous trap. The Centre for Social Justice has carried out extensive research demonstrating the link between welfare dependency and long-term job prospects, family breakdown and mental health problems.[24]

Perhaps the most significant social dimension is intergenerational. As David Willetts argues in *The Pinch*, if one generation works less for more benefits, it simply builds up more debt for future generations.[25] In 2010, the National Institute for Economic and Social Research estimated that a failure to tackle the national debt would leave each born now with an additional tax burden of £200,000 over the course of their lifetime.

In a globalised economy, the work ethic matters even more. Those countries with a stronger work ethic will have a sharper entrepreneurial edge. Their companies will be better at competing for international business. Those countries will be more likely to attract foreign direct investment. For all the talk of rebalancing the UK economy in favour of manufacturing and industry, British labour has been systematically priced out of that market. When it comes to large-scale manufacturing and heavy industry – as opposed to high-tech niches – it is too expensive in the UK to hire the workers to make things at an internationally competitive price.

Take the example of the semiconductor industry. The world's leading manufacturer of semiconductors is the American company Intel, which designs and manufactures most of its chips in the US.[26] Intel chips formed half of the so-called 'Wintel' model that dominated computing in the last 20 years: Microsoft made their Windows software, and Intel produced the chips that it ran on. The future, by contrast, looks increasingly set to be dominated by the more power-efficient ARM chips that run devices such as iPhones, iPads and Windows 8 tablets. Over 95 per cent of smartphones run on ARM.[27] ARM is a British company, based in Cambridge, but unlike Intel, it only designs rather than manufactures its chips. While Intel largely builds its chips in its home country, ARM's chips are shipped out of American and Asian factories.

Why Bother?

So, fewer Britons are working fewer hours, with major economic and social implications. But what is driving this trend? Two causes stand out: high tax rates and a poorly designed welfare system. For those without a job, generous benefits make it harder to motivate themselves to find a job. By contrast, those in work are put off from working any longer than they have to by the excess size of their tax bill.

In 2005, economists at the Harvard Institute of Economic Research found a strong correlation between tax rates and aggregate hours worked. Between a third and a half of the extra hours Americans work they attributed to the lower level of US taxation.[28] A further US study of 19 countries including Britain, over a period dating back to 1977, found clear evidence of the chilling effect that rising tax rates – payroll and consumption – have on the number of hours worked.[29]

Since 1992, the share of net taxes as a percentage of GDP in Britain has increased by 5 per cent. This is mirrored by a 5 per cent fall in average working hours over the same period.[30] Since 2005, there has been a sharp increase in income tax at all levels. Those paying income tax at the lowest rate have seen the share of their earnings taxed rise by 20 per cent, whilst millionaires have seen a 28 per cent rise.[31]

The correlation between rising tax rates and decreasing working hours makes sense. If it pays less to work, more and more will come to the view that it is not worth the effort. Beyond the dampening effects of taxation, the Harvard Institute also found that short working hours were associated with high levels of unionisation. Looking at all the countries in the OECD, the economists concluded that '[t]he bottom line is that hours worked fell in countries that can be characterized by the Continental European model and did not fall in countries with the American model (with Britain and Ireland in between)'.[32] This is perhaps best summed up by the comments of one Scottish entrepreneur, 'I have built up a world leading position in our field. We employ about four hundred people. I work twelve plus hours a day. I find paying the 50p tax demoralising. Sometimes I feel "why bother?".'[33]

Through tough bargaining the unions have successfully increased the amount their members are paid, and reduced their working hours. Union militancy in Britain has got worse since the Harvard study. In 2005, Britain lost 157,000 working days to strikes. In 2011, Britain lost 1,373,200 working days to strike action – 93 per cent of which were in the public sector – the greatest number since riots over the poll tax in 1990.[34]

There is also overwhelming evidence that we need to work for longer. The Old Age Pensions Act in 1908, creating the modern pension system, set the pension age at 70 for both genders. When the contributory system was created in 1926, the age was lowered to 65. However, male life expectancy was 76 years compared to 86 years today. If the state pension age had risen according to life expectancy, it would be at least 75 now. Under the government's reforms, the state pension age will rise to 66 by 2026 and 68 by 2046. That will not stop an increase in the number of pensioners of 2.5 million by 2030.[35] In terms of the cost to the taxpayer, expenditure on public sector pensions has increased by a third over the last decade to £32 billion. In terms of fairness, even after reform, public sector employees will enjoy the benefit of 'career average salary' pensions. These are out of reach for the majority in the private sector who are paying for the pensions in the public sector.

Overall, 40–45 per cent of adult lives are now spent in retirement compared to roughly 30 per cent in the 1950s. The balance between the years we spend in work and the years we spend in retirement has grown unbalanced. So, while the Unison union bemoans the 'Great Pension Robbery', the reality is that their campaign to frustrate pension reform would be socially unjust, by loading up more debt or higher taxes for the next generation to pay off.

A further factor undermining the British work ethic is the rise of welfare dependency. The postwar welfare state was designed as a safety net to help the poorest and most vulnerable. It has ballooned beyond all recognition, corroding the UK work ethic. Based on research into European unemployment levels, Jean-Baptiste Michau at the London School of Economics argues that 'the expansion of the scope and size of the unemployment benefits system that occurred after the Second World War decreased the returns from having a strong work ethic'.[36]

In Britain, there has been a massive rise in welfare dependency. The generosity of income support has risen sharply since the war. In today's money, the taxpayer now spends ten times more on social security than in 1950 – with a fivefold rise in the number of people claiming unemployment benefits. The number of people claiming sickness and disability benefits has increased thirteenfold.[37]

In 2011, there were 5.7 million people of working age claiming benefits. The lion's share of these, about 4 million, comprises those seeking work (1.4 million) and those deemed incapable of working (2.6 million). Recent Work Capability Assessments conducted by the Department for Work and Pensions found that 57 per cent of those assessed for sickness benefits were fit for some sort of work.[38] The British state has made it too easy for too many people to take the easy option. This was never the intention of the postwar Labour government.

Worse still, state dependency in Britain actively defers people from working. A YouGov poll in 2008 found that just a quarter of benefit claimants thought they would be better off from working; 39 per cent were convinced they would be worse off if they worked harder.[39]

As the Centre for Social Justice has documented, for too long work has not paid. The loss of benefits from taking up a new job has been as great as any gain in wages. Welfare dependency has created a glass ceiling that prevents climbing the employment ladder. For one single mother interviewed, Jane, taking into account the withdrawal of benefits, 75 per cent of her increased earning potential would be offset by the loss of benefits, resulting in a negligible economic incentive to take on a job.[40]

Another growing cost to work is the burden from childcare. Childcare costs have risen for each year over the last decade. Twenty-five hours of nursery care for a child aged two or under costs an average of £5,000 per year, rising to £6,000 in London. Parents in Britain face higher childcare costs as a share of net income than any other country in the OECD, spending an average of 33 per cent of net income on childcare.[41]

One reason for the higher costs is that Government has increasingly added to the regulatory burden for childcare. Informal and cheap childminders are increasingly being replaced by heavily regulated nurseries. In 1997 there were 100,000 childminders, making up half of all formal childcare. By 2011, there were just 55,000 childminders, only 15 per cent of the market.[42] Those childminders that are left are faced with Ofsted requirements for compulsory registration, mandatory staff–child ratios and a detailed curriculum. The sheer hassle of the bureaucracy, paperwork and inspections has caused thousands of childminders to quit.

Research for Save the Children and the Day Care Trust found that a quarter of parents, irrespective of income, reported that childcare had caused them to get into debt.[43] The costs of childcare equate to 41 per cent of mortgage or rent payments. For those in poverty, a quarter had given up work and a third had turned down jobs mainly because of the high costs of childcare. The marginal extra income from work is now so finely balanced with the cost of childcare that it is deterring many on lower and middling incomes from returning to work. Research for the insurance giant Aviva shows that, after tax, a woman in a relationship on the average part-time salary of £8,557 with children aged one and seven would lose £98 a month by going back to work.

Delayed Gratification

In 1972, psychologist Walter Mischel of Stanford University conducted a 'marshmallow test' with four- to six-year-olds at a nursery, and the results were followed up with further studies between 1988 and 2011.

The children were offered one marshmallow straight away, or two if they waited a while. Just one third could avoid the temptation, and waited long enough to get the second marshmallow. The follow-up studies showed a striking correlation between those who passed the test, and educational results and wider measures of life attainment. Being able to make a sacrifice and defer gratification with a longer-term goal is a powerful trait that holds children in good stead.

There is a growing consensus among experts that the prospects for youngsters are decided very early in life. If they do not get the right start, it is difficult to claw back lost time. For many young Britons, their life chances will have been significantly determined by their teenage years.

Take Tuggy Tug, standing on a rough street corner in Brixton, waiting for people to mug. At 15 years old, his problem is not lack of ambition. Far from it. He readily talks through his 'five-year plan', during which he wants to make as much money as possible through violence and drugs, and then go 'legit', buy a home in the suburbs and even learn to play golf.[44] For most 15-year-olds, having a five-year plan of any description would be a sign of maturity. But, the get-rich-quick attitude is more likely to leave Tuggy Tug in prison or dead, according to statistics. His attitude reflects poor primary school education. He says the teachers didn't care whether he was there or not. There was little discipline from his parents. Brought up by a single mother, she never disciplined him, because he was bringing home so much cash – up to £200 per day from a life of petty crime. As for deferred gratification, the cost-benefit analysis of a life of crime points all one way: if he followed more legitimate methods, he complains, he'd be a pensioner before he saw real rewards.

Compare Tuggy Tug to Jessie Tang, a British-Chinese A Level student in Watford.[45] Her father works in a takeaway restaurant and her mother at Heathrow airport. Jesse won twelve GCSEs including six A*s and plans to read music at university. Asked about the secret to the marked success of young Chinese students in Britain, she points to the high expectations her parents have of her.

Many families in the Indian community also recognise the link between hard work and success. The Hinduja brothers, who own businesses in a number of sectors, talk of how their attitudes to business and aspiration have been passed down from their father, with one commenting that they 'hope their father's values have been passed on to a new generation'.

A similar story comes from Britain's richest man, Lakshmi Mittal. He always aspired to do business, starting off by helping to run his father's steel business in India whilst he was out of college. He turned his aspiration into enterprising spirit by setting up his own factory and kept his entrepreneurial spirit alive, consistently building upon and expanding his businesses. He is now CEO of ArcelorMittal, the largest steel company in the world.

Mittal's rise from family business to global success is not a one-off. His story is common in many Asian families. Many in the Asian community have set out as entrepreneurs to build a better life for themselves and their families. Families would often make sacrifices to ensure the success of their next generation, and many British businesses run by members of the Asian community have received finance from their owner's relatives to enable them to start up. The older generations are willing to make these sacrifices to foster the desire and will to succeed in their younger generations. Many have attributed this work ethic to the 1960s, when Asian immigrants to Britain who had very limited possessions and no welfare state entitlements would only have one way to turn. They relied on hard work and, in essence, entrepreneurialism, to realise their burning ambition for a better life.

If parental values are an important foundation in nurturing a strong work ethic, schools ought to see it as their role to strengthen it further. Yet a 2005 Ofsted report found that almost half of people in their twenties said their education had not prepared them for their first job. Two-thirds responded that more could have been done to prepare them for the world of work. Around half felt that their education had not put enough emphasis on bread-and-butter skills like attention to detail and meeting deadlines.

The attitudes instilled in the classroom translate into the workplace. Research by the Centre for Social Justice in 2011 found that despite rising unemployment, JobCentres are notified of a quarter of a million vacancies every three months.[46] A further Manpower Talent Shortage Survey between 2009 and 2010 found it was increasingly difficult to fill roles such as chefs, waiters and hotel staff. The Centre for Social Justice argues that on top of schools' focus on the three Rs – reading, writing and arithmetic – a new emphasis on 'responsibility' is needed to encourage children to take greater ownership of their lives, citing an employer survey that showed that 82 per cent of entry-level employers rated attitude and work ethic as important to progression versus 38 per cent for literacy and numeracy. The top reason for turning down job applications – at 62 per cent – was also poor attitude and work ethic, followed by poor presentation (at 57 per cent) and lack of work experience or practical skills (at 38 per cent).

The Confederation of British Industry has set out a range of practical proposals to plug the 'employability gap'. These include promoting work experience while still at school, expanding apprenticeships and vocational training. They also advocate welfare reform to remove the perverse financial incentives not to take work.[47]

In 2011, UK youth unemployment hit 1 million. Despite the tough economic climate, academic research is increasingly concluding that the level of Jobseeker's Allowance is still actively encouraging the unemployed to be more fussy about which jobs they are prepared to do.[48]

One young jobseeker, Cait Reilly, took matters further. Reilly graduated from her Geology degree at Birmingham University in the summer of 2010. Her long-time ambition is to work in the museum sector, but by the autumn of 2011 she still hadn't managed to find a job. As a condition of receiving £53 per week on benefits, she was required to attend a two-week placement, stacking shelves for her local Poundland. This, she argued, in January 2012 while suing the government, was a breach of her human rights. Forcing her to work, her lawyer argued, was nothing more than an 'Orwellian' scheme,[49] a breach of Article 4(2) of the Human Rights Act: 'No one shall be required to perform forced or compulsory labour.'[50]

Role Models

If indifferent parenting and mediocre schooling have contributed to an erosion of the British work ethic, some argue it has been further exacerbated by an increasingly pervasive celebrity culture. Instead of celebrating the connection between hard work and success, we instead fixate on 'undiscovered talent' in the arts, or a single 'eureka' moment in business. As the cliché goes, most overnight success has years of preparation behind it. Even the best new business idea is worthless without the right execution. The British are still too obsessed with the idea of the gentleman amateur.

In 2009, Sky television channel Watch commissioned a survey of 3,000 families with children aged between five and eleven years. It asked about the dreams and ambitions of the children compared to their parents. The top three careers the children aspired to were sports star, pop star and actor. Twenty-five years ago, the three favourite careers had been teaching, finance and medicine.[51] Three-quarters of parents complained that the media was the single biggest influence on their children's ambitions in life. In response to the survey, child psychologist Lavern Antrobus warned that while children were often shown the glamour of celebrity life, the long years of hard work that lay behind success were far less obvious.[52]

In December 2011, Welfare Secretary Iain Duncan-Smith went further still, linking the celebrity culture and the luck-over-work attitude it conveys to the urban riots of August 2011.[53]

Reality television is increasingly blamed for creating delusional expectations and encouraging youngsters to want to be footballers' wives (the so-called WAGs) or make a career out of a soap-opera lifestyle, like ex-page 3 model Katie Price.

In truth, some reality television emphasises the high-risk, hard-working nature of working life at the top. Few would begrudge the eventual winners of the gruelling series *The Apprentice* for seizing their opportunity to work for no-nonsense entrepreneur Lord Sugar. Even the much-maligned *X Factor* is all too willing to expose – sometimes harshly – those with a poor work ethic or lousy attitudes, with the 'Judges' regularly stressing the competitive nature of the industry and the importance of a good work ethic. Likewise, for every one successful pitch on the *Dragons' Den*, there are hundreds of failed ideas. Many of these shows offer a glimmer of hope that someone from an unconventional, humble or just an untrained background can 'make it'. But they are also fiercely competitive.

One 'Dragon', Hilary Devey, left her Bolton school at the age of 16. She was a single parent, who remortgaged her home and sold her car to enable her to set up a distribution business in an extremely male-dominated sector. Having started with no investment other than her personal belongings, the odds were firmly stacked against her. However, her aspiration and hard work led to resounding success and she is now the Chief Executive of the UK's number 1 palletised freight distribution network, with a turnover approaching £100 million. She is a role model for young entrepreneurs and an example that it can be done.

Clearly, not all reality television is the cheap exhibitionism of *I'm a Celebrity Get Me Out of Here* and *Big Brother*. Equally, there are few sports personalities who reach the heady heights of David Beckham without years of monotonous hard graft. The extent to which the celebrity culture simply reflect, rather than shapes wider cultural attitudes is also open to debate. In truth, it is probably a bit of both. But blaming the superficiality of the celebrity culture should not become a substitute for tackling a far deeper problem.

People will always be attracted to shortcuts that offer a rapid ascent to fortune and fame. In interviews, Lord Sugar often makes the point that young entrepreneurs too often expect the one in a million success of Mark Zuckerberg's Facebook, rather than the hard grind of most business.[54]

He is equally quick to lambast what he calls the 'cushy' benefits system for generating an 'expectancy culture'.[55]

Sugar is an example of a dwindling breed of self-made UK entrepreneurs who started out from modest beginnings, with few qualifications, and built up businesses to be internationally competitive.

Sugar was born in 1947, the youngest of four children. From a young age, he worked hard to raise his own money: getting up at 6am to boil beetroots for a local greengrocer,[56] selling factory discards to the rag-and-bone man, brewing ginger beer, doing a milk and paper round.[57] By the time he left school, at 16 he was earning far more than his father, who as a tailor earned just £13 a week.[58] In 1967, he started his own business, selling aerials out of the back of a van. He soon moved into his own manufacturing, and by the 1980s his company was doubling its profits every year.

But how realistic is he as a role model today for youngsters growing up in twenty-first-century Britain?

Rags-to-riches stories have become less prevalent in the UK, because social mobility has fallen since the war. The scope for children born in 1958 to climb the economic and social ladder was much higher than for those born in 1970. The sharp decline has tapered off, but social mobility – at least that which can currently be measured by educational attainment – has not recovered, despite the billions of public money invested in state education in recent years.[59] According to a survey in 2010, the earnings of British children correlated more strongly with their parents than in any other country in the OECD.[60]

The drivers of social mobility remain hotly disputed. Some argue that greater inequality of wealth was behind this, while others point towards welfare dependency and the curbing of grammar schools as explanations. However, one factor is clear. Fewer Britons work. Those who work put in fewer hours. For the overwhelming majority, the financial rewards from hard work have declined because of higher taxes or perverse disincentives in the welfare system. Standards of state education have fallen, leaving fewer avenues for the brightest from modest backgrounds to succeed. There are also fewer economic and social incentives for those who might otherwise make that difficult journey based on hard work.

All the evidence points to a decline in the work ethic in Britain. This is reflected in UK industrial relations, law, tax, welfare, schooling, parenting and wider social attitudes. This phenomenon is not uniform or consistent. There are wide discrepancies in attitudes to work that cut across the public and private sectors, the professions as well as communities. Nevertheless, the overall trend is stark. A decreasing number of people, working fewer hours, are expected to shoulder the responsibility for an increasing minority who are wilfully not working.

This is not a sign that our economy is doing better. The UK is falling behind in competitiveness and there remains a lingering productivity gap. Nor can it be justified as the price of a fairer society. Social mobility has stalled, youth unemployment has reached record highs and inequality has widened.

Above all, Britain finds itself increasingly ill-equipped to take on the hungry and ambitious international economic competition from Asia to Latin America. These trends will surely continue unless we rediscover the lost virtue of hard graft.

5 Buccaneers

If Britain is to invent the companies of the future, we will need to be prepared to take more risks. Britain can learn from the entrepreneurial culture of Israel and Silicon Valley's ability to embrace failure.

Giffords

On 8 January 2011, US Representative Gabrielle Giffords was shot in the head from point-blank range by gunman Jared Lee Loughner, in the car park of a Tucson supermarket. Eighteen others were also shot, six of whom died, in an act of appalling violence. Astonishingly, Giffords survived her wounds, in part due to the heroic actions of her staffer Daniel Hernández Jr and emergency services personnel. But there was also another factor that may well have provided medical responders with the crucial edge, one that originated 7,500 miles away in Lod, Israel.

Bernard Bar-Natan was serving as a military medic, in 1980s Israel. He discovered in the course of his training that the bandages issued to combat haemorrhaging were based on a 1942 design. He was appalled to think that technology in this most vital area did not seem to have advanced for 40 years.

> Weapons had advanced since World War II, medicine had advanced since the 1930s; it seemed to me that the personal field dressing and the treatment for haemorrhage control should also advance.[1]

Bar-Natan came up with a bandage with an inbuilt bar to apply direct pressure – the key to staunching blood flow from a wound. His idea had two main goals: stopping the bleeding without inadvertently effecting a tourniquet, and making a bandage that could be used on all parts of the body – cutting down the amount of equipment needed to be carried.

I 'worked' on the ideas on and off for a couple of years, sometimes not touching it for months, but it wouldn't leave me. I made a few rough prototypes by myself and with the assistance of a local tailor for the sewing part. I began to show the concept to other medics in my unit, and to doctors in the military; no-one said stop.[2]

Bar-Natan persevered, and took advantage of a technology incubator programme. Once he had successfully been granted a patent, he managed to obtain further investment, established First Care Products and then began factory production of his 'Emergency Bandage'. He did not successfully make a sale until 1998[3] when Belgian and French forces used his bandage in Bosnia.

I established the company in 1995, our first sales were to French and Belgian NATO forces in Bosnia in 1998. We gave away many bandages to the USA, and European countries, Israel for their evaluation and to create the awareness; small quantities were sold. We started with the special forces and medical corps. When the US went to Afghanistan and Iraq the first times, the bandage went with them in small quantities, but enough to make an impression. In November 2003 they were designated 'Standard' by the US Army, and larger size orders began at the end of 2004, in 2006 for the IDF, and September 2007 for the British Army.[4]

This story of invention and persistence in the face of adversity – from a man with no history in business – culminated in the bandage being adopted by the IDF, the US Army, and the British Army, as well as being the de facto standard for many others. This is despite the geopolitical sensitivity in some parts of the world to a product that has become widely referred to as the 'Israeli Bandage'. It is the archetypal story of a driven entrepreneur – willing to take risks at every turn, particularly with his own money. As Bar-Natan himself puts it, 'Funding first must come from your own pocket – there is no better motivator.'[5] Success very seldom comes overnight.

Bernard Bar-Natan's 'Israeli Bandages' were in the standard first aid kit used by paramedics from the Sheriff's office in Pima County that responded to the Giffords shooting. Though the chaos of that day has left some details obscured, it seems likely that Bar-Natan's bandage saved lives in those vital first minutes after the attack. Bar-Natan told us that when police first arrived on the scene they did not know how many shooters there were. As a result, half of them began to provide emergency first aid, and the others started to secure the site – on the basis that they had no way of knowing whether or not it was safe for paramedics to operate. The horrifying injury sustained by Representative Giffords is exactly the sort of trauma that his bandage was designed to treat.

The connection between a frustrated IDF medical trainee and an assassination attempt in Arizona tells us something of the nature of invention. This was a small yet vital improvement with the potential to save lives, which grew out of the unique entrepreneurial environment of Israel. Success has many fathers – and none more so than in the case of this particular bandage. It can be explained by factors as varied as a particular Yiddish colloquialism, a revolutionary package of free market reforms, a government-sponsored incubator programme and, of course, an IDF medic puzzled by the lack of progress in trauma technology.

Every country has its share of star innovators – such as Bernard Bar-Natan or James Dyson – but Israel enjoys more than most. Despite its small size and lack of natural resources, Israel has the highest number of tech start-ups outside of the US and the third highest number of companies listed on the NASDAQ. Israel has the highest amount of venture capital attracted per capita in the world, three times the level in the US, and 30 times the average in Western Europe. Israel's 7 million workers attract as much venture capital as France and Germany combined.[6]

Many countries have tried to grow their own version of Silicon Valley, but Israel is one of the few to succeed. Twenty years ago, Israel was famous mostly for farming and defence technology. Now, executives at Google and Microsoft regularly point to 'Silicon Wadi', the area around Tel Aviv, as the second most important in the world for tech start-ups. *The Economist*[7] and industry magazine *Wired*[8] agree.

What is it that the Israelis are getting so right?

Israel – *Chutzpah*

Nearly everyone who works in an office environment will be familiar with the need to transfer files quickly and securely. The USB flash drive has become an invaluable part of daily life for millions of people. No more carrying around bulky disks, simply insert a thumb-sized flash drive, small enough to be carried on a key ring.

What is less well known is that this vital piece of technology did not emerge from one of the American or Japanese powerhouses of innovation. Instead, it was an Israeli company, M-Systems Ltd, that developed and patented the first flash drive (known as DiskOnChip) in 1995. It also developed the first USB flash drive (DriveOnKey) in 1999 and the True Flash Filing System which allows a flash drive to appear as a disk drive to a computer's operating system.

Take another piece of quotidian technology – instant messaging. Millions of people are able to communicate with each other in the blink of an eye, all over the world. Indeed, for many young people it is a service that is almost as vital as their mobile phone. The first internet-wide instant messaging service was the still operating ICQ, created in the mid 1990s by the company Mirabilis, the intellectual progeny of five innovative Israelis. Two years after its launch, Mirabilis was bought by the American telecoms and media behemoth AOL for $407 million, the most lucrative ever sale of an Israeli tech company at the time.

This track record of innovation and enterprise shows no signs of abating – in 2010 the growth rate of patent applications in Israel was 7.90 per cent; in the UK, by contrast, there was a decrease of –2.40 per cent.

This success is reflected in the wider economy as well, Israel being one of the last countries to enter recession and the one of the first to leave – growth in 2010 averaging 4.5 per cent, significantly higher than the OECD average of 2.7 per cent.[9] A 2008 OECD report on science and innovation also showed Israel as spending a higher percentage of GDP on research and development than any other country – 4.53 per cent.

Such is Israel's reputation for innovation that in December 2011, Apple announced that it is to open its first research and development centre outside of California – in Herzliya, Israel.[10] This R&D centre will join dozens of others set up my multinational companies, including Google, IBM, Microsoft, Intel, Motorola and Hewlett Packard, each trying to tap into the Israeli genius for innovation.

The idea of national character influencing economic success is a well-used one, in the case of Israel it is encapsulated in the terrific Yiddish word *chutzpah*. A district court in the US once defined this as 'presumption-plus-arrogance such as no other word, and no other language can do justice to'.[11] The classic legal definition is of a man who murders his mother and father, then throws himself on the mercy of the court on account of being an orphan. There is no direct English translation, but it is this audacity and rejection of deference that is found time and time again in the history of Israeli entrepreneurship. Though traditionally a somewhat damning term, in the context of risk and bold business acumen it takes on a more admirable note. There is a distinct cultural tendency amongst successful entrepreneurs to challenge conventional wisdom, and act with daring to exploit new opportunities. This does seem to dovetail perfectly with the *chutzpah* that is displayed by Israel's most inventive start-ups.

Table 5.1   Growth rate of patent applications at top 20 offices, 2010

China	24.30%
European Patent Office	12.27%
Singapore	11.97%
Russian Federation	10.20%
Israel	7.90%
US	7.50%
France	5.70%
Australia	5.10%
Republic of Korea	4.70%
Australia	4.47%
Brazil	3.47%
Italy	2.80%
Mexico	2.10%
DPR Korea	0.60%
Germany	−0.60%
Japan	−1.10%
China, Hong Kong SAR	−1.30%
UK	**−2.40%**
Canada	−5.47%
India	−6.97%

From Oranges to Apple

It is impossible to undersell the importance of the technology sector to Israel's economy. In 2000, a third of Israel's exports came from the IT sector. Until the software boom that began in the late 1980s, the most productive sectors of Israel's economy were more akin to that of a developing nation. Exports relied on cut diamonds and agriculture – predominantly Jaffa oranges.[12] Though it would be misleading to characterise Israel's economy at this stage as entirely primitive, it hardly seems the most promising basis for a modern innovation-led economy.

Of course, Israel's technological sector did not spring unbidden from the ground in the 1980s. The success was a culmination of decades of a culture that celebrated scientific innovation. From the earliest days of an independent Israel, science was at the forefront of the economy, and of course the all important national defence. Academic Daniel Isenberg points out that this impetus came right from the very top, with Presidents Chaim Weizmann and Ephraim Katzir both coming from a scientific background.[13] However, the Israeli economy cannot be said to have truly flourished until the 1990s. As late as 1985 the country was suffering from hyperinflation, reaching 445 per cent at one point. A strict programme of economic reforms, including liberalisation, curbs on deficit spending, and high interest rates managed to stem the tide. The Economic Stabilisation Plan, cutting spending and devaluing the shekel, reversed what appeared to be an inevitable decline following the Yom Kippur War of 1973 – and is a telling example of the benefits of fiscal discipline from the state. For despite the instincts that may have driven entrepreneurial endeavour, the early State of Israel was also hampered by a risk-averse state, with high job security and limited competition. This combination merely led to stagnation. Until the 1980s, innovation was stifled by a welfare state that celebrated caution and shied away from risk taking. It is clear, then, that it is not just the people that inspire a country. The right political and economic culture is also needed.[14] While recognising that it is the market, not government, that is ultimately responsible for success, judicious government policies can act as a catalyst in certain circumstances. In Israel's case, this has taken two complementary forms, the Technological Incubators Program and the Yozma programme. Both of these stand-out successes can be attributed to Yigal Erlich, Chief Scientist of Israel's Ministry of Industry and Trade from 1984 to 1992.

Israel's government-backed Technological Incubators Program is a model for sensible government support for entrepreneurship. It does not attempt to pick winners or subsidise doomed ventures. Its stated goal is to raise private investment for as many companies as possible, offering seed capital for companies that have the potential to soon become viable and raise money on their own. It also deliberately seeks out high-risk, innovative enterprises at an early stage in their development, recognising the potential rewards on offer. The programme operates on an annual budget of $35 million, which is mostly distributed in small increments of around $600,000. At any one time, the 26 separate incubators collectively support around 200 projects. The idea is to transform high-risk ideas into viable investment opportunities for private backing.

Mission statement – Technological Incubators Program

The primary goal of the program is to transform innovative technological ideas, that are too risky and in too early stage for private investments, into viable startup companies that after the incubator term are capable to raise money from the private sector and operate on their own.

Each incubator operates as a private legal entity, on a for profit basis. This removes the government control typical of British industrial policy in the past.

Bernard Bar-Natan describes his experience of an Incubator Program:

You must prepare a business plan including a budget for each year detailing what you are going to do with the money. If the budget is accepted, the Government puts in 80 per cent, the entrepreneur must make up the additional 20 per cent ... If the project succeeds and there is revenue, the funding is categorised as a loan and must be paid back, +3 per cent. If the project fails, the funding becomes a grant ... The [incubator] staff act as mentors and assist with procedure and business practices. It will also assist in looking for next-stage funding, after the two-year period.

The incubator itself receives between 15–20 per cent of the shares in the company established.[15]

Venture capital did not really percolate into the Israeli economy until 1993, when Yigal Erlich persuaded the government to launch the Yozma program. As Chief Scientist at the Ministry of Trade and Industry, Erlich was in charge of an annual $200 million budget to support research and development at technology companies. He soon found himself disappointed with the results. While Israel's talented scientists were skilled at creating new technologies, they were much less good at marketing their new products. Israel simply didn't have the necessary cluster of investors, firms, talent and mentorship needed to create a new tech hub. Most foreign investors were understandably not keen on investing in a small, distant, and war-torn country, whose economy was only just recovering from decades of oversized government.

The Yozma program was crucial in offering a lure to foreign investors to bring both their expertise and money to Israel. In effect, Erlich hoped to import the best of Silicon Valley to Israel. The Government allocated $100 million to create ten new venture capital funds, each of which would be a partnership between an Israeli bank, an Israeli venture capitalist and a foreign venture capital firm. The Government would put up 40 per cent of the capital as long as the private sector could raise the other 60 per cent. Investment decisions would be made by the venture capitalists, avoiding the charge of 'picking winners'. After five years, the investors were given a cheap option to buy out the Government, and eventually nine out of the ten funds were to do so. This allowed Yozma not only to cover its costs, but also to return a profit to the Israeli government of around 50 per cent.

Such was the success of Yozma in creating a venture capital industry, where previously none had existed, that it was allowed to come to a natural end. By the end of 1990s there was 60 times more invested by Israel's venture capital firms than there had been at the start. Between 1991 and 2000, the number of companies launched by venture funds rose from 100 to 800. The government determined that there was enough private investment available to make its contribution redundant. Yozma was privatised in 1997.

This is particularly telling when you compare it to the British experience of government subsidy. In Britain, by contrast to Israel, businesses have a tendency to melt away once the tap of taxpayer cash is turned off. A perfect example of this flawed approach in the UK is the system of feed-in tariffs, which acted to subsidise a solar energy sector. Energy Minister Lord Marland laid out the stark figures – £7 billion spent for £400 million of net present value.[18] A viable industry should not require that level of public subsidy in order to function. Remember, the brilliance of the Yozma programme lay in the success of its enterprises. These enterprises went on to be successful and economically viable. They were not merely parasitical. Israel also ensures that its foreign policy takes into account the needs of Israeli enterprise, to identify potential markets and partners abroad.

One additional factor arrived in the 1990s, in the form a million Jewish immigrants from the former Soviet Union. These new arrivals had a high level of technological and scientific education. With this influx of talent, Israel effectively imported a class of highly skilled innovators. The antipathy towards individual enterprise that typified the sclerotic Soviet Union, along with deep-rooted antisemitism, fuelled a population shift of unparalleled importance. It was estimated in 2009 that immigrants from the former Soviet Union represented half of the high-tech workers in Israel.[19] It is not too much of a stretch to suggest that the sort of people inclined to travel thousands of miles to a small, isolated, desert country – without even knowledge of the language – might possess exactly the sort of boldness that scientific discovery relies upon. Binyamin Netanyahu declared that this influx of talent 'rescued' Israel, and should be treated as 'one of the greatest miracles that ever happened to the state'.

Consider too, that all this success comes from a country of just 7.8 million people, surrounded by often hostile states and geographically isolated from major world markets. This lies behind the nature of Israeli tech companies. They predominantly cater to other businesses. This is confirmed by the marketing executive Yonatan Sela,[20] who points out the difficulty in constructing a consumer brand. Compare this to the UK, with its large, affluent population and ready access to Europe; the potential gains from a flourishing culture of enterprise ought to dwarf those of Israel.

Of course, it may be that this need to improvise due to scarce resources itself leads to successful innovation. If, as Malcolm Gladwell would have it, a successful product requires 'threat and constraint', Israel would seem to be the ideal proof of this.

Perhaps, then, part of the secret to Israel's success lies simply in demographics and geography. Either way, the Israeli miracle shows what can be achieved when the right to take risks is set free.

Fear of Failure

By contrast, Britain is becoming an increasingly risk-averse society. This is most visible in the growth of what might be termed the health and safety industry, but its pernicious effects intrude into all sorts of corners of our national life. Sociologist Frank Furedi writes compellingly about a culture of fear, which undermines the natural human impulse to take risks. He claims that as a culture we increasingly feel powerless in the face of risk, giving in to a worst-case thinking that has become an organising principle of public life.[21]

The effect that this has on enterprise in Britain is demonstrated by the regulations that hinder business. For example, the fear of unemployment and unfair dismissal has led to a system of employment law that discourages small business from taking a risk and hiring new staff. A ComRes poll in 2010 suggested that 57 per cent of people felt 'employment law provides too much protection to employees who perform or behave badly at work'.[22] This lack of flexibility in staffing arrangements can be overcome by a large corporation, but for a small business, it is crippling.

Over the last 30 years, employment regulation has gone up by 502 per cent. This amounts to an economic burden of £112 billion, just to comply with red tape.[23] It is equivalent to 7.9 per cent of the GDP of the UK – or the entire output of Singapore. An extra £23 billion in costs is predicted by 2015. Naturally, it is upon small businesses that the burden falls the heaviest. These firms simply do not have the resources or manpower to keep abreast of the avalanche of regulation inflicted.

A British Chamber of Commerce survey from June 2011 showed that one in three small business owners surveyed who were considering expansion were put off by costs of complying with the new National Employment Savings Trust Scheme. The same proportion said they *would* expand if given exemptions to these rules. It is estimated that over 80 per cent of small firms use external expertise to help them comply with employment regulation, as they are unable to afford to appoint full-time compliance officers.

The World Economic Forum's league table of regulation has the UK ranked at a poor 83rd – down from 51st in 2005. It should be a matter of intense alarm that, in a difficult economic climate, the burden has increased on businesses. This is not even merely a matter of political will – it can be attributed to a much deeper cultural problem. The tendency to insist that 'something must be done' by the government, every time a company fails, is rooted in the culture of fear.

According to responses in the *Global Competitiveness Report 2011/12*, the top five most problematic factors for doing business in the UK are tax rates, a lack of access to financing, inefficient government bureaucracy, regulation and inflation. These are all symptoms of a swollen, cosseting state, in which risk aversion has become embedded as a central principle of government.

This is borne out by the number of days it takes to start a business in the UK – 13. This compares to only a day in New Zealand and two days in Australia, countries that are comparatively similar to us. Why does starting a business in those countries only require a single procedure, where in Britain it takes six?

The Government's idea of enterprise zones is definitely a step in the right direction. However, these do not go as far as some of the Gulf States, such as Dubai. The Jebel Ali Free Zone was the first and largest 'free zone' created in Dubai. It offers the best tax incentives in the world. It also offers the facilities for companies to set up there. Incentives such as freedom from corporate and personal taxes are available for businesses in the short term and can be renewed if necessary. Regulation is kept to a minimum. Companies within the zone are not subject to import or export duties. The success of the 'free zone' can be seen by the diversity of international businesses investing in Dubai. The infrastructure is in place for companies to invest with full confidence that internet, telecoms and transport infrastructure are all there. This investment in infrastructure and lack of regulation binding businesses has helped Dubai to be recognised as a hub for business in the Middle East.

There are other grounds for optimism for the UK. The survey used for the *Global Competitiveness Report 2011/12* ranks Britain's scientific research institutions behind only Israel and Switzerland for quality.[24] We also score very highly on the collaboration between universities and industry in research and development. It is clear from this that much of the necessary infrastructure is in place. What is lacking is the willingness to take risks.

Black Market Buccaneers

An interesting side note on the question of risk and innovation is the so-called 'informal economy'. This is estimated to have a collective value of $10 trillion.[25] Robert Neuwirth's *Stealth of Nations: The Global Rise of the Informal Economy* makes the bold claim that this motley collection of enterprises have a great deal to teach the rest of us.[26]

Neuwirth estimates that half of the workers in the world are part of this shadow economy. The black market operates at the purest level of entrepreneurialism, untouched by law, regulation or tax. Predominantly a feature of the developing world, the business model of creating low-quality, low-cost products and selling them to equally poor people might not seem to be something that we would want to emulate.

What this demonstrates is a fairly basic correlation between innovation and regulation. We have seen in the past the effects of a centralised, over-regulated state – the Soviet Union. It had little capacity to properly supply the needs of its people. With the informal economy we see the other side, a lawless place where demand can be instantly met by supply, in its rawest, most elemental form. For example, Neuwirth tells us that it was underground Chinese manufacturers that first offered a dual-sim-card mobile phone. It was sold through street vendors in countries where mobile phone provision works on a patchwork basis.[27] This is something that can now be bought in a perfectly legal way, but it was the informal economy that got there first. The market abhors a vacuum, and it is the smaller, more nimble enterprises that can fill them, long before a multinational leviathan like, for example, Nokia, can even begin to contemplate developing a product.

In some of the world's most dynamic developing economies, such as Vietnam, we see capitalism as chaos, a maelstrom of scooters, hawkers and makers, each scrapping to turn a profit. Economist Le Dang Doanh estimates that in Vietnam the private sector currently constitutes 40 per cent of GDP, on top of which exists a further 20 per cent which can be considered the 'underground' economy.[28]

Clearly, law and order, intellectual property rights and consumer law exist for a reason, and are on the whole beneficial. But as a sheer experiment in what the poorest entrepreneur can achieve, when nearly all society's strictures are relaxed, the informal economy is pretty hard to beat. The tradeoff between risk and reward is more visible here than anywhere else. As Steve Jobs once famously said, 'It's more fun to be a pirate than to join the navy.'

Frontier Spirit

The conceit that Britain ought to play the wise cultured Athenian to the boorish new Romans of the US is an old one, and not without its charms for those still nostalgic for empire. But in 2012, where many commentators are writing about the decline of the West, and looking to the rise of China, India and Brazil – will it be necessary to recast our relationship with America? More than this – will it be necessary to become more like them?

The frontier spirit animates all that made the twentieth century the American Century. An independent spirit, unrestrained by central regulation, inspired an unprecedented transformation. From humble beginnings in 13 largely agrarian states in 1776, the USA expanded into the most dominant economic powerhouse that the world has ever seen.

Of course, there were certain natural advantages – resources, space and climate. And as a former British colony America benefited from a legal and political system that crucially emphasised freedom and property rights. American institutions both reflect and preserve the national character of self-reliance and aspiration, stemming from the clarity of the Declaration of Independence and its inalienable rights to 'Life, Liberty and the pursuit of Happiness'.

It is the third of these that is the most profound. America's founding charter offers the guarantee that citizens have the right to pursue happiness, rather than guaranteeing happiness. This is an important distinction. Contrary to the typical modern statism, that is risk-averse and cosseting, this declaration is an *active* idea. It makes clear to American citizens that happiness is in their hands and within their own power to attain.

Thomas Jefferson described the Declaration of Independence as 'An expression of the American mind.' The following two and a half centuries have shown this to be true. From the frontier myth of the pioneers, to the capitalist ethos of the Gilded Age, taking that leap into the dark has been central to America's image of itself.

Americans have always been relentless in reinvention, refusing to just accept mediocrity on the grounds of 'that's how it's always been'. A disregard for the conventional wisdom and curiosity about the new and unknown is hardwired into the DNA of every great inventor.

Risk, Failure and Invention

It is often said that necessity is the mother of invention. If that is so, one might well posit that the father of invention is failure. Thomas Edison famously said 'I have not failed. I've just found 10,000 ways that won't work.' Similarly, the story of every bold inventor or entrepreneur follows an identifiable template, with failure and setbacks experienced and then overcome. These failures are often essential, not just in building character but in improving the final product. If Britain is to invent more of the products of tomorrow, it must be unafraid to first fail faster and earlier.

The right to fail, and then try again, is enshrined in American law through the regulations surrounding bankruptcy. Since 1898, the right to file for Chapter VII or Chapter XIII bankruptcy has been available to all US citizens, described by economic historian Niall Ferguson as 'one of the distinctive quirks of American capitalism'.[29] Chapter XI bankruptcy is available to businesses for the purposes of reorganisation.

Much of this is about mindset, perception and culture. Where a company becomes insolvent in the UK, this is often seen as a failure. The US has a far more relaxed attitude. English law in particular is designed to protect creditors, with sanctions and even criminal liability in place to target directors of insolvent companies. In the US, by comparison, filing for bankruptcy is frequently a business strategy. It allows entrepreneurs to cut their losses, pick themselves up, and start again.

This refusal to stigmatise failure is a core American principle, and has much to be admired. In the UK it would more often than not be replaced by bitterness, recrimination, and dark mutterings about the nature of capitalism.

Perhaps the archetypal example of British expat creative success is Steve Jobs' right-hand man, Jonathan Ive. Ive was born in Chingford at 1967, but left London in 1992 to move to California and take up a position at the computer giant. While at Apple, he designed perhaps the most influential gadgets of the last 20 years: the iMac, the iPod, the iPhone and the iPad. When asked in early 2012, what made him make the move, he told reporters that it was California's sense of optimism, the ability to play with ideas without fear of failure.[30]

Clearly, the examples of Lehman Brothers, General Motors and Enron suggest that failure and bankruptcy are not without their downsides. As journalist Tim Harford suggests in his 2011 book, *Adapt: Why Success Always Starts with Failure*, the key is to make sure that failure is survivable.[31] In the early stages of a project, failure need not be a disaster.

Of course, none of this is news to those who live and breathe enterprise. There is an annual conference in San Francisco – Failcon – which is devoted to learning the lessons of trying and failing, specifically in the tech industry. At this conference, entrepreneurs both budding and successful meet to discuss their experience of failure and in particular the way in which failing ultimately led them to succeed. Failing fast is the best way to learn how to 'pivot' to tomorrow's success. Intuit, a company that specialises in accounting software, even goes so far as to hold 'failure parties'.[32]

Lex Deak, a British entrepreneur who sold his first business at the age of 25, says:

> In speaking with tech colleagues in the States one gets a different response to new venture discussions. The tone of conversation is much more positive. [The] focus is on the opportunity, the market size ... and who might be interested in getting involved. In the UK I have noted time and time again that the slant is much more cautious with focus on the downside, competitors, challenges in getting to critical mass and ... how tough it is going to be to raise investment ... Across the pond entrepreneurs seem to embrace failure, it is seen as a prerequisite to success and worn as a badge of honour. In the UK ... failures hold you back like a weight around your neck.[33]

Since 1 January 1997, the number of UK companies incorporated then subsequently dissolved follows the time frame shown in Figure 5.1.

A total of 61,495 companies were dissolved within a year, 1,954,571 between one and five years, 486,407 between five and ten years, and 62,489 after more than ten years. While it cannot be calculated for sure how many of these companies traded before being dissolved, the statistics do suggest that failure is an elemental part of business.

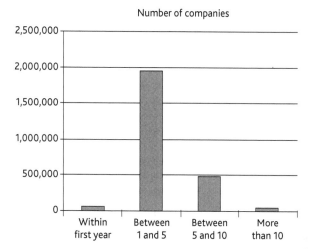

Number of companies

Figure 5.1

Silicon Valley

Silicon Valley in California is the centre of the IT universe, It is where innovative tech start-ups vie for venture capital, and where technological titans such as Twitter, Google and PayPal were all born. It is without a doubt the most visible modern manifestation of the pioneering, entrepreneurial American spirit.

There are a number of elements to Silicon Valley's success – which explains the difficulty that other countries have had in trying to emulate it. Firstly, the proximity of Stanford University, a world leader in science and technology, offered a steady stream of highly skilled graduates in the decades following the Second World War, closely backed by local businesses such as Hewlett Packard. This is not in itself unique of course; after all, Britain is hardly bereft of world-class universities. A number of other factors have been studied, including, but not limited to, a high-skilled workforce; a creative, risk-taking culture; complementary legal and financial institutions, and the high quality of life.[34]

So Silicon Valley benefits more than anything from a ready access to venture capital – which allows for the harnessing of risk in the interests of innovation. Sand Hill Road has become as synonymous with private equity investment as Wall Street is with the stock market. Each year, billions of dollars are invested in new start-ups – capitalism in its rawest, most primordial form. Instead of the tinkering around the edges of enterprise zones, or government-subsidised green technology, we see the unrivalled power of the market in picking winners and backing innovation.

According to PriceWaterhouseCoopers, in the third quarter of 2011 $6.952 billion was invested by venture capital into private emerging companies in the US. Of this, a staggering $2.67 billion went to companies based in Silicon Valley and its environs – 38 per cent of the total amount. This investment in start-ups is beneficial to all involved. In fact, last year average annual salaries at technology companies in the area topped $100,000 for the first time.[35] At a time when the outlook for the global economy remains fragile, the power of free market capitalism to improve the quality of life for workers is unique.

This resilience was also present after the collapse of the dot com bubble between 2000 and 2002. A recent study showed that, contrary to popular belief, the entrepreneurship rate was actually higher during the six years following the NASDAQ's peak than in the boom years of the late 1990s.[36] It was the recovery in high-tech growth following the dot com bubble that was the engine of regional growth in America, from 2003 to 2008.

Peter Mandelson himself attributed the lack of a British Google, Amazon, Microsoft or Apple to a shortage of venture capital. In 2009 he claimed that only 4 per cent of UK investment goes to venture capital, compared to 33 per cent in the US. Though the UK venture capital market is notably larger than that of continental Europe, it remains paltry compared to that of the US. A 2009 report from the BVCA argued that the UK venture capital market had simply not reached the critical mass yet to adequately fund companies.[37] In terms of venture capital availability, the UK ranks a weak 23rd, with Israel, by comparison, in second place.[38]

It is this access to private capital that allows so many American business start-ups to grow and flourish. Though funds are incredibly selective about their investments, ultimately each investment is a gamble based on risk versus reward. The influential academic Daniel Isenberg, a specialist on what is needed to grow an entrepreneurial environment, describes this as the most vital feature of an 'entrepreneurial finance ecosystem'. If healthy, the system should be as willing to deny capital to ventures that do not deserve it as it is to allocate capital to a venture that does. This intelligent approach to risk means that in a system essentially built around taking chances, the odds are going to be stacked in the investor's favour.

It is not just venture capital funds that take risks on investing outside of traditional banking structures. Successful founders often invest their newfound wealth into the next generation of start-ups, combining mentorship and money in a new role as an angel investor. Members of the so-called 'PayPal Mafia' have gone on to invest in YouTube, Facebook, LinkedIn, SpaceX, Zynga and Flickr, among many, many others.

A similar model seems to be emerging in Wenzhou, China, home to 140,000 companies, and considered the home of Chinese enterprise culture. Small businesses frequently found themselves struggling to find loans from Chinese banks, who prefer to lend to the larger state-backed enterprises that typify the Chinese model of capitalism.[39] So instead, entrepreneurs in Wenzhou turned to each other for loans to grow their businesses, building a thriving market for private credit, providing credit in places where state enterprise would otherwise suffocate small and medium enterprises. The Chinese government estimated in 2011 that 60 per cent of businesses in Wenzhou used some form of private lending.[40] Significantly, this is not economic success underpinned by government subsidy. In 2005 the BBC reported that over 95 per cent of the local economy was based in the private sector.[41]

Worryingly, patent applications appear to be trending downwards in the UK. This is especially worrying because of the propensity for increased innovation during downturns illustrated by the example of Silicon Valley. The number of national patent applications has declined from 17,484 in 2006, to 15,490 in 2010. At the same time, however, more patents are being successfully granted, as Table 5.2 shows. Perhaps this demonstrates a quality-over-quantity approach. Or, paradoxically, perhaps it is desirable to see more patents rejected, since innovation can be measured by the number of attempts that fail, as well as those that succeed. Returning to Isenberg, he suggests that 'hyperentrepreneurial' countries see a great deal of early failures. These failures demonstrate where opportunities may or may not exist. It is a form of creative destruction that has much to recommend it. Isenberg's point is that policy-makers should not treat low failure rates as a sign of success, rather there should be a great number of success and failures alike – though naturally with a clear emphasis on the former.

Patents in the US are expensive – both in terms of money and time. It takes around two years for a patent to be approved or rejected. Most inventors employ the services of a patent lawyer to ensure that their idea has not already been claimed. The total cost of this process is estimated at around $10,000 a time.[42] There is, however, also a basic protection that lasts for just one year, with a price tag of $105, which can give an inventor time in the short term.

Table 5.2   Patents granted by region

Region	2006	2007	2008	2009	2010
East Midlands	128	96	109	114	111
East of England	371	284	272	302	288
London	524	316	361	292	382
North West	254	187	167	192	201
Northern Ireland	13	11	10	11	7
North East	82	33	32	37	41
Scotland	138	130	117	127	169
South East	607	428	411	421	472
South West	344	207	212	209	244
Wales	88	62	60	67	66
West Midlands	234	149	159	167	163
Yorkshire	150	125	132	146	141
Postcode not given/Incomplete address	45	30	28	33	38
Total	2,978	2,058	2,070	2,118	2,323

Predictably, there is a strong regional variation in patents granted, with the South East, London and the East of England, the home of Cambridge University, consistently out-performing other regions.

If you compare the number of patents granted in the twelve UK regions with the most 'inventive' US towns you get a depressing picture. According to a 2005 study conducted by iPiQ on behalf of the *Wall Street Journal*, each of the ten most inventive towns were granted more patents in 2005 than any single British region. San Jose topped the chart with 3,867, dwarfing even the total British number of 2,978. Eight of the top ten are situated in California.[43]

On a national level, the US's greater population explains the disparity in successful patent applications. Looking at the performance of individual towns, however, suggests failure on the part of the UK to complete at the top level. It is impressive enough that eight of the ten most inventive towns in the US are in California – predominantly in Silicon Valley. But when you consider that the UK has twice the population of California, this really begins to illustrate the gulf that presently exists.

Unsurprisingly, there also appears to be a strong correlation between innovation, employment and turnover. Table 5.3 provides estimates for the number of companies in each region, organised by turnover.

We can see from this that where successful companies flourish, they do so always with innovation. Success breeds success. It is in areas where the record on innovation is poor that fostering an enterprise culture can have the most impact. The experience of Silicon Valley shows that the economic situation does not stifle innovation. Talent is easier to find, the competition is less fierce, and creative thinking is at a premium in difficult times. The demise of British heavy industry in areas like the North East has left them economically deprived, but this should not be treated like a death sentence.

All of this raises the question, 'If they can do it, why can't we?' After all, there's no shortage of inspirational examples of British entrepreneurs; James Dyson, Richard Branson and Peter Jones instantly spring to mind. Nor can the UK succumb to the quick and easy temptation of statism – that more government spending is the answer. Corporatism has little to recommend it. The malaise lies deeper than government policy alone can address.

Reid Hoffman, founder of LinkedIn and one of the most famous Silicon Valley venture capitalists, argues that there is no reason why you couldn't replicate the Valley's success in Europe. One area in which Britain is already competitive with the US is the quality of its universities. If Silicon Valley was originated from and is sustained by graduates of Stanford University, Hoffman argues that London, Oxford and Cambridge could allow Britain to become the entrepreneurial centre of Europe. While Cambridge may never be able to overtake San Francisco, second place is still a position well worth having. Take the example of California's other world-famous hub: Hollywood. The British film industry is in no danger of overtaking America, and yet has nevertheless thrived for decades. Many of film's most famous franchises have been filmed in British studios: not just Harry Potter or James Bond, but also Star Wars, Indiana Jones, and Pirates of the Caribbean.

Table 5.3 **Number of companies by region**

Turnover (£ millions)	1 < 5		5 < 10		10 +		Total	
	2010	2011	2010	2011	2010	2011	2010	2011
Region								
North East	3,270	3,080	515	505	605	545	**4,390**	**4,130**
North West	12,700	12,105	2,110	1,990	2,265	2,095	**17,075**	**16,185**
Yorkshire & The Humber	9,525	8,825	1,590	1,455	1,700	1,565	**12,815**	**11,850**
East Midlands	8,725	8,235	1,350	1,195	1,455	1,400	**11,530**	**10,830**
West Midlands	10,865	10,105	1,670	1,445	1,805	1,695	**14,345**	**13,245**
East	13,085	12,290	1,985	1,850	2,225	2,130	**17,295**	**16,270**
London	23,810	22,885	4,120	3,910	5,425	5,160	**33,355**	**31,955**
South East	19,930	18,730	2,965	2,775	3,610	3,455	**26,500**	**24,960**
South West	9,650	9,190	1,350	1,270	1,335	1,300	**12,335**	**11,755**
Wales	4,005	3,830	620	565	630	590	**5,255**	**4,985**
Scotland	7,825	7,365	1,325	1,245	1,485	1,385	**10,635**	**9,995**
Northern Ireland	3,290	3,140	605	550	580	540	**4,475**	**4,235**
Total	126,680	119,780	20,205	18,755	23,120	21,860	**170,005**	**160,395**

Already, there are promising signs of an organically growing start-up scene in London's Silicon Roundabout and Tech City. There are now an estimated 5,000 technology companies in East London.[44] While none has the importance of a Google or a Facebook, Last.fm, Songkick and TweetDeck are genuinely global brands. Swedish music company Spotify has chosen to locate its head office in London. A busy schedule of hackathons, meetups and pitching days are helping cement the entrepreneurial culture. Sequoia Capital, a venture capital firm which has previously backed LinkedIn, Zappos and Airbnb, has just made its first investment in the UK. New crowdfunding solutions like Crowdcube and Seedrs are making it easier to access seed capital. The new Seed Enterprise Investment Scheme offers some of the best tax incentives for initial investment in the world.

There is nothing in the British national character, no flaw in the British people, which would prevent us from excelling in the same way as Israel or America. The burdens of regulation and red tape are solvable. It is a particular mindset that must be engendered. Embracing risk and taking responsibility must beat its core. Samuel Johnson said that 'courage is reckoned the greatest of all virtues; because, unless a man has that virtue, he has no security for preserving any other'. This is as accurate an epigram for the entrepreneurial mindset as any.

What the US and Israel can teach us is that when it comes to innovation, the underlying *ethos* is all important. It doesn't matter how many natural advantages there are. It is the entrepreneurial mindset which is needed for success. This is not to say that such a thought process cannot be learned. What is clear is that if Britain's future is to be built on high-tech innovation, as is widely assumed, complacency will not be an option. When you consider that the value of the internet in the G20 alone is predicted to reach £2.7 trillion by 2016, we cannot afford to 'play it safe'. It is the freedom to take risks, fail and try again that underpins capitalism.

Britannia Unchained

Whereas countries like Japan and Germany suffer from a shrinking, aging population, Britain is experiencing a new baby boom. We should learn from the optimism of growing countries like Brazil, and be assured that our best days can still lie ahead. Rather than growing old and comfortable, Britain must be prepared to think like a young country, ready to work hard and to take risks.

> For so long, Brazil was a nation brimming with potential but held back by politics, both at home and abroad. For so long, you were called a country of the future, told to wait for a better day that was always just around the corner. Meus amigos, that day has finally come.[1]

So said President Barack Obama in his speech to 2,000 Brazilians on his tour of Latin America in March 2011. Just that morning Obama had toured the once-violent Cidade de Deus slum, made infamous by the 2002 film *City of God*. Now he stood in the crowded Theatro Muncipal, an elegant theatre of gold trim and red velvet.[2] To rapturous applause, he concluded, 'This is a country of the future no more. The people of Brazil should know that the future has arrived.'

Obama was hardly telling the Brazilians something they didn't know. A poll in January 2011 showed Brazilians to be the most optimistic people in the world, with 78 per cent expecting their local economy to improve in the next six months. India came second at 61 per cent, while just 25 per cent of people were optimistic in the United States. In the United Kingdom, the figure was a mere 12 per cent. At the bottom of the list, a dismal 4 per cent of the French were optimistic about the future of their country.[3]

Even politicians are popular in Brazil. The last leader, President Lula, still enjoyed an 80 per cent approval rating after eight years in power,[4] leading Obama to describe him as 'the most popular politician on earth'.[5]

Lula was born to poor, illiterate parents in 1945 in the small city of Caetés in north-eastern Brazil. He himself didn't learn to read until the age of ten. As a child, he worked as a peanut seller and shoe-shiner. Later, he trained as a metal worker, and, after the death of his first wife in 1969, became increasingly involved in trade unionism. In 1980, he founded the Workers' Party, Brazil's first major socialist party. After three unsuccessful attempts, he finally won his election in 2002. Despite concerns that he would turn back the country's economic progress, once in power he proved more moderate than some of his radical 1980s rhetoric. On his original election in 2002, financial markets panicked, fearing debt default and a reverse of economic reform, but by his re-election in 2006, they had calmed down. During his presidency, over 20 million people were lifted out of poverty. At the end of his constitutional two terms in 2010, he stepped down.

After her first year in office, Lula's successor and Brazil's first woman president, Dilma Rousseff, enjoyed her own approval rating of 70 per cent.[6] She also started on the left of politics. She began her adult life as a Marxist guerrilla, and in 1970 was captured and tortured for two years by the then military dictatorship.[7]

The Brazilians have much to be optimistic about. The Brazilian economy was one of the last to enter the global recession, and one of the first to exit. In December 2011, Brazil overtook the UK to become the sixth largest economy in the world. According to the Centre for Economics and Business Research, the Brazilian economy will soon overtake France and Germany as well.[8] Recent major discoveries of oil could help turn the country into a major exporter of the fuel.[9] After one of the steepest drops in the fertility rate ever seen, from 6.2 children per woman in 1964 to 1.8 in 2010, the country's dependants ratio has improved considerably and the population has stabilised. In the 1990s there were 90 dependants, the large majority children, to every 100 adults. The ratio is now 48 dependants to every 100 adults. This allows the country to focus more resources on improving quality rather than quantity in relation to public services.[10]

The next four years will see the world's attention focused on Brazil as never before. Brazil will host the Olympics in Rio de Janeiro in 2016. In 2014, the world's most successful national soccer team will bring the tournament home, staging the FIFA World Cup.

Nowhere is the turnaround in Brazil's fortunes more obvious than in the changes in the once infamous favelas. To the outside world, mention of the favelas summons up images of desperate poverty, ramshackle houses and lawless crime. Inside the favelas, however, the young residents are increasingly optimistic about their future.

Brazil's shantytowns date from the late nineteenth century, the first favela created in the 1890s by 20,000 veteran soldiers after the Government refused to pay them. The favelas really grew in size, however, in the mid twentieth century, as more people left the countryside to look for work in the city. While life is difficult in the favelas, their residents are still far richer than those left behind in the country. Around 9 per cent of those in Rio de Janeiro's slums live on less than a dollar a day, below the World Bank-defined poverty line. The equivalent proportion in the rural north-east is 55 per cent.[11]

What is worse is the level of crime. Without legal title, many of the favelas lacked not only basic infrastructure, but any state authority. The police and ambulances refused to cross over into the favelas. Taxis and delivery vans would not enter them. The drug lords filled the power vacuum.

To some extent, the drug lords created their own miniature state, even able to impose their own curfews. One foreign scholar, Simone Beuchler, recalls negotiating directly with the gangs to gain access to slums for her research. The drug lords agreed, to an extent – letting her visit, but telling her that if she wasn't gone by six at night, she'd be killed.[12]

The drug lords' peace, however, was unfortunately only maintained when the gangs were not at war with each other, or the police. As many as one in five people from Rio's favelas have lost at least one family member to the drug war.[13]

In 2008 the Brazillian government began a campaign to retake control of the favelas, creating a new Police Pacification Unit (UPP). In many ways, the operations of the UPP are closer to that of an army than a traditional police operation. Armoured personnel carriers and bulletproof helicopters mount a 'shock and awe' invasion, regaining control of the streets and driving out the gangs. Once authority is restored, specially trained community policemen move in to keep order and provide basic services such as healthcare, sanitation and electricity.

By 2011, 19 favelas had been 'pacified'. In November, Rocinha, the largest of Rio's favelas, was reclaimed after an operation involving 3,000 troops in a night-time raid.[14] The once-feared drugs kingpin

Antonio Francisco Bonfim Lopes (or 'Nem') was caught trying to escape in the boot of car.[15] A further 21 UPP operations are planned by the time of the Olympics.[16]

Even before the pacification process, many of the residents of the slum had shown they possessed entrepreneurial instinct. Despite the hard life they have been brought up in, they are confident that with hard work and initiative they can secure a better future. Their optimism about the future of their community helps support their own personal aspirations.

Many, such as 20-year-old Mayara, are starting up their own tour companies to show tourists around the favela.[17] Despite still living with her parents and two sisters, she already has plans to start her own bed and breakfast and tourism agency. She hopes that the coming attention during the Olympics will be a chance to change the world's perspective on Brazil and the favelas.

Certainly, there are many role models Mayara could look up to, in fields from fashion to professional services.

A resident of the Barreira do Vasco favela, Silvinha Oliveira, has created her own fashion label. She uses donated scraps from clothing factories to produce a range of sandals, handbags and accessories.[18] Recycled plastic bottles donated from the community are used to create the packaging.

Another entrepreneur, Edivan Costa, spent his childhood in the favelas scavenging scrap paper and selling it to local recyclers to pay for his school books.[19] After seeing the difficulties businesses had in keeping up with Brazil's legendary red tape, he decided to set up his own professional services company, Sedi. If it takes on average 150 days to set up a new company in Brazil, Sedi boasts that it can speed up the process to just 30–40 days – all without paying any bribes.[20] In 2008, Sedi's revenues topped $7 million, and its clients have included Unibanco, Carrefour and C&A.[21]

Leila Velez, Ernst and Young's Entrepreneur of the Year in 2006, is co-founder of Beleza Natural, a beauty salon dedicated to black hair.[22] Growing up in a Rio favela, Velez realised that a product for frizzless hair would be hugely popular. Despite no scientific training, she managed to come up with an effective formula through repeated experiments on a generous husband. She sold a VW Beetle for $3,000 of initial capital, and started a salon. The company soon expanded, as Velez applied the best-practice management techniques she had observed in a teenage job at McDonald's. Every aspect of the business has been carefully tested, perfected and codified. The company tries to help its employees better themselves, having negotiated 30–50 per cent tuition discounts at local universities. Despite no outside financing, the company now has 26 salons, each serving up to a 1,000 customers a day.[23]

Brazil has long had the potential to be one of the world's leading nations. In terms of land area, the country is over 35 times as large as Britain. It is roughly half of South America and includes around 60 per cent of the Amazon rainforest. Near 200 million people live in it, making it the world's fifth most populated country. Since 1950, when the country was the same size as the UK, the population has quadrupled. Most of these people are relatively young, with the median age under 30.

The twentieth century was a frustrating experience for Brazil. In the political arena, the country flitted between democracy and military dictatorship. A military coup in 1889 deposed Brazil's second (and last) Emperor, Pedro II, inaugurating 40 years of democracy. A second coup in 1930 led to rule by a military junta under Getúlio Varga until 1945, before democracy returned for a brief 21-year period. In 1965 the military once more took power, fearing that Brazil would otherwise follow Cuba's path to Communism. The military regime finally handed over control in 1985, and the first direct elections were held four years later.

Economic growth proved similarly unstable. In the years after the Second World War, the economy converged with the West, growing at an average of nearly 7 per cent a year between 1945 and 1980.[24] In the 1980s the model of state-led industrialisation reached its limit, after the Latin American debt crisis caused Brazil to lose access to international capital markets. In order to pay its debts, the Brazilian Government turned to printing money. The result was hyperinflation that regularly reached over 2,000 per cent a year.[25] This phase only ended when the Government created a new currency, the Real, pegged to the dollar, in 1994. By the beginning of the new millennium, the economy was growing strongly again, but the experience had taken its toll on convergence with the West. In 1980, Brazilian GDP per person was 28 per cent the American level. By 2011, it was only 20 per cent.[26]

Many problems still remain in the country's economy. The country is still one of the most unequal in the world, despite the rise of a growing middle class. A quarter of the population live on $100 or less a month.[27] The gangs remain a serious problem, and the murder rate is one of the world's worst. You are nearly 20 times more likely to be murdered in Brazil than in the UK.[28]

The so-called 'Brazil cost', discouraging international businesses from investing in the country, remains high. Infrastructure is poor, with underdeveloped roads and overcrowded ports. Excessive bureaucracy, a convoluted tax system and significant corruption create further problems. Altogether, according to the World Bank's rankings, Brazil is one of the worst countries to do business in, coming in at 127th out of 183 countries.[29] Brazil's education system is very poor, and the country scores badly on the international PISA rankings.[30] Interest rates remain high, a legacy of culture that learned in the years of hyperinflation to avoid savings. Brazilian workers are not yet as efficient or hard working as their Asian competition. Terry Gou, Chief Executive of Foxconn, the manufacturer of Apple's iPad, complains that 'Brazilians, as soon as they hear "soccer," they stop working. And there's all the dancing. It's crazy.'[31]

Even more seriously, there are worries that some of the problems of the 1980s could return. There is only so long that a country can grow through simply investing more capital, especially if it is funded by outside debt. As the Soviet Union discovered in the 1950s, and the East Asian economies in the 1990s, a country eventually has to transition to growth from increased innovation and productivity rather than mere investment.[32] Between 2002 and 2008, productivity grew a rate of less than 1 per cent annually in Brazil, compared to an average 4.6 per cent in the US.[33] This will have to change if the current growth performance is to prove sustainable.

Yet, despite these problems, the young Brazilians remain relentlessly optimistic. They are proud of their country, and looking forward to a bright future. Brazilians are much less likely to emigrate from their country than many other nationalities. There are only about 250,000 Brazilians living in the US compared to 2 million residents from El Salvador, despite that country's population being a 30th of the size.[34] In 2000, just 2 per cent of Brazilians with a university education chose to leave the country to live somewhere else.[35]

It was French President Charles de Gaulle who, perhaps apocryphally, after a state visit was said first to have said, 'Brazil is the country of the future ...' Unfortunately, he also added the snide

'... and always will be'.[36] Now to the Brazilians it seem that the first half of de Gaulle's jibe is coming true. The economy is booming, politics is settling down, and even the lawlessness of the favelas is being conquered. No wonder so many of the young are optimistic about the future, and keen to work hard to prosper. To Brazil, it seems that their best days can only lie ahead.

Young Country

In Britain when you turn 100, you receive a congratulatory letter from the Queen. In Japan, the Government sends a memorial silver sake cup. When the tradition was established in 1963, the Government sent out cups to just 153 centenarians,[37] but Japan has aged since. The Japanese Government now sends out 20,000 cups a year. Worst for the recipients, in order to save money, the Government had been forced to cut silver in each cup from 94g to just 63g.[38]

The world is growing older. In both developing and developed countries, the number of children is shrinking and the number of pensioners growing. In the short term, the baby boomers are just hitting their retirement. Welfare policies everywhere created in the booming mid century are proving unsustainable. In the long term, we will all have to either work longer or save more.

In the 1950s, almost every country had a ratio of at least five workers to each retiree. China had 11.6 workers, France 5.1, Japan 10.0, the US 6.9 and the UK 5.6. By 2050, much of these differences will have been eliminated as almost every country is predicted to have a ratio of around two workers per retiree. China's ratio is predicted to be 2.4, France 1.9, Japan 1.2, the US 2.6 and the UK 2.4.[39]

Nowhere is aging faster than Japan. By 2060, life expectancy is predicted to be 90.93 years for women and 84.19 years for men.[40] As many as four in ten of the Japanese will be over 65.[41]

Neither are the Japanese having babies. Birth outside of wedlock remains rare – just 2 per cent of babies are born to single mothers – but the age of marriage has been steadily rising.[42] A combination of Japan's fierce work ethic and modest support for childcare leads many to put off marriage and children while they focus on their jobs.

A country's fertility rate is measured by the expected number of children born to the average woman. For a population to remain stable, each woman has to produce exactly one daughter each. In practice, that works out at a fertility rate of just over two. Japan's fertility rate is already just 1.39, and expected to be 1.35 by 2060.[43] The result is that Japan's population is expected to shrink by a third in the next 40 years.

Next door to Japan, China faces its own problems with aging. The legacy of China's one-child policy is the demographically fatal 4–2–1 family structure: four grandparents, two parents, one child. Enrolment at primary schools has already dropped from 25.3 million in 1995 to 16.7 million in 2008.[44] In the next decade, the number of people aged 20–24 will drop by a half.[45] The share of people over 60 will double in the next 20 years.[46]

In Europe, Germany is likely to see its population drop from 82 million today to 65 million by 2060.[47] The Germans, too, are putting off marriage, and struggling to combine family and work, especially when many schools still close at midday. Until recently, measures by the Government to boost population were taboo, bringing back bad memories of the Third Reich's Mutterkreuz medals, awarded to women with four or more children.[48] On the other hand, Germany's benefits and regulatory system are much more family-friendly than other developed countries with higher birth rates, such as the US. Germany's problem is as much cultural as political.

Germany's birth rate is now the lowest in Europe, at 1.38 children per woman.[49] The number of Germans under 18 has declined by 2.1 million in the last decade.[50] By 2030, every retiree will be supported by just two workers.[51] One expert, Harald Michel of the Institute for Applied Demography, has even gone so far as to claim that Germans are at risking of dying out.[52] This is almost certainly not going to happen, but Germany will shrink.

And yet, surprisingly, the UK is predicted to grow.

In common with the world as a whole, the fertility rate in the UK began to fall sharply in the mid 1960s. As women moved into the workplace, the contraceptive pill became more widespread, and education and wealth increased, birth rates dropped everywhere. By the mid 1970s, the trend levelled off, at a fertility rate of around 1.8 – a rate at which it stayed for much of the rest of the century.

And then at the beginning of the millennium something strange happened: UK fertility rates began to rise again.

In 2010, there were 723,165 new babies in England and Wales, 2.4 per cent more than in 2009, and a massive 22 per cent increase from the 594,634 births in 2001.[53] Fertility rates have risen every year for a decade, until they are now at the crucial 2.0 level – for the first time since 1973.[54] In 2011, Tesco reported a 31 per cent increase in sales of pregnancy tests.[55]

While the number of pupils in Germany is going down, in England the Government expects that they'll need an extra 450,000 places by 2015.[56] Some schools in London are already so busy that they are looking at a shift system: one set of pupils attending from 8am to 2pm, and the other set from 2pm to 7pm.[57] Manchester is predicted to experience a rise from 37,000 primary school pupils now to 46,000 by 2015.[58]

Nobody is quite sure exactly why Britain is experiencing a new baby boom. The ONS suggests that improved support for childcare and migrant mothers both helped.[59] Mothers are now also happier having their babies older. Many are now catching up with earlier decisions to put off childbirth. While the number of teenage mothers or those in their twenties has fallen, the number of babies born to the over-40s has tripled in the past 30 years.[60] In the last ten years alone, the number of births to the over-30s has gone up by 22 per cent.[61]

As the whole world ages, Britain will remain a relatively young country. Past experience suggests that this can only be healthy. More young people means more minds to create new ideas and generate wealth, more opportunities and creativity, and more help to look after the old. Much of the growth of the mid twentieth century across the world came from a 'demographic dividend', as the population surge from the baby boomers reached the workplace and helped drive the rest of the economy.

Imagine the experience of someone born and growing up in the internet age. They are at ease in a globalised world, as used to discussing last night's TV with friends from Hong Kong as Hereford. Twitter doesn't care what country you come from, or 'Call of Duty' where your fellow 'soldiers' are really located. They are used to a digital world of near infinite choice, greater transparency, and careful personalisation, where gatekeepers and intermediaries everywhere are fast going out of business. They are used to a world in which the West can no longer lazily assume its own superiority, but instead has to work harder to compete with a developing world that is fast catching up. At the same time, hang-ups over issues like Empire or national decline can seem little more than ancient history.

The new generation of Britons are proud of their country. In survey data, they are only marginally less likely to claim pride in British citizenship than the wartime generations of the retired – and they are much more optimistic about its future: 54.6 per cent of the over-65s believe 'Britain's best days are behind her', while two-thirds of those aged 18–24 disagree.[62]

They are more liberal as well, and less statist. According to British Social Attitudes survey data, support by the young for greater tax and spend peaked in 1991. It has been in the decline ever since. While the majority believe that the state is about the right size, a growing minority think it should shrink. In 1987, just 2 per cent of the 18–24s believed taxes and spending should be cut. By 2010, it was 10 per cent. In 1987, 49 per cent believed that the Government should redistribute income compared to 31 per cent who disagreed. By 2010, opinion was exactly divided on the question, with 35 per cent agreeing and 35 per cent opposed. Support for greater welfare benefits halved between 1997 and 2010, from 52 per cent down to 26 per cent – the likely reason being that the young increasingly believed that benefits prevented the poor from learning independence. In 1987 just 23 per cent agreed that 'if welfare benefits weren't so generous, people would learn to stand on their own two feet'. By 2010, 54 per cent agreed.

Unfortunately, the new generation is often being held by the baby boomer Establishment. Despite their often cynicism about Britain, the 'Ben Elton' generation has done very well out of the postwar years. It is the young that are now paying for the legacy of their parents' overregulation and overspending. The ladders that allowed their parents to succeed – rigorous education, a liberalised economy, a housing boom – have been pulled away, or moved out of reach. Some of the boomers not only don't recognise their good luck, but seem actively hostile to helping the next generation – you might call them the 'baby busters'.

Perhaps the best recent example of the baby buster mindset is an article by Joan Bakewell. Bakewell, once memorably described as the 'thinking man's crumpet', has had a long London-based career as journalist, television presenter and Labour Party peer. Born in 1933, Bakewell is technically one generation older than the height of the boomers, but she shared many of their advantages. 'Some 48 years ago, as young marrieds, we scoured London for rundown properties which had potential', she recalls. 'I favoured tall ceilings, big windows. I didn't need a garden but I did want trees and a view of grass. We ended up paying £12,000 for a house in a decrepit London square, painted the front door olive and started a trend. Over the decades and with no effort on our part, the area has been transformed and so have the prices. Houses in the Primrose Hill area fetch well over a million these days and are snapped up by pop stars, TV chefs and hedge fund managers.'[63]

Despite Bakewell's self-admitted belief that she bears little responsibility for the increase in value of her home and her claim that 'I am all for taxing the rich more', she is unsurprisingly against any attempt to share any of this windfall through the tax system. The aging baby busters are all for increased taxes on the successful and hard working to keep generous pension systems afloat; they are against any increased burden on their own wealth or house values.

If he were bright and hard working, a child born just after the Second World War could enjoy education at a rigorous grammar school, followed by university paid for by the taxpayer. Favourable demographics will allow him to do well from the welfare state – over his lifetime the generation will take out approximately 118 per cent of what they put into the welfare state.[64] He would emerge from free education into a booming economy, where good jobs were easy to find. He would likely be able to afford a house of his own, and the inflation of the 1970s would help erode the value of the mortgage. In 1968, 425,000 new houses were being built a year. Restrictive planning regulation ensured that that number dropped until, by 2010, despite a larger population and smaller families, just 100,000 houses were added.[65] The shortage in supply led to a decades-long boom in property prices, adding to our baby boomer's wealth. The value of many houses rose by over 100 per cent in real terms.[66] Our baby boomer can look forward to a long retirement, based on estimates of life expectancy nearly a century out of date. Most of his universal benefits remain ringfenced by the government, while his defined benefit pension is unlikely to ever be experienced by his children.

While most baby boomers continue to thrive, many of the young are struggling to find work. For the first time, the living standards of those in their twenties have slipped below those in their sixties. Britain has the fastest rise in the OECD in older people's income compared to the young. More than 80 per cent of Britain's £6.7 trillion wealth is held by those born between 1946 and 1964.[67] Between 1995 and 2005, those aged between 25 and 34 saw their wealth fall, while those between 55 and 66 saw it tripled.[68] One in five boomers owns a second home.[69] By contrast, just 15 per cent of owner-occupied housing is owned by those under 44.[70]

That is not to say that quality of life is irretrievably in decline, or that, as some such as former Chancellor Alistair Darling say, 'You can't honestly say to younger people any longer, you'll do better than your father or mother's generation.'[71]

As we will see, there are real advantages to a relatively young, dynamic population – and Britain has a huge opportunity for the future.

Country of the Future

The Brazilians are so optimistic because they think their best days are ahead of them. The British are often so pessimistic because they believe that their best days are behind.

But they need not be.

Even the most daunting of obstacles, changing a whole culture, can be achieved with enough political determination. Meiji Japan moved from isolated feudalism to a modern economy in two generations. Under the leadership of Mustafa Kemal Atatürk, the remnants of the Ottoman Empire transformed into the nation of Turkey. Those countries imported the best of Western technology, education and culture and succeeded in turning their future path around.

Rather than transform its entire culture, Britain must only regain respect for its own traditions and confidence in its future. Rather than growing old and comfortable as its institutions stagnate, it must be prepared to think like a young country, ready to work hard again.

The British lack confidence in who they are, but arguably no other country has given so much to the world. The British have overspent badly in recent years, but the examples of Australia and Canada show that is it possible to keep finances under control. The British education system has stagnated, but still contains some of the best universities and schools in the world to build on. The British are working less hard than they used to, but pockets of work ethic still exist among the industrious taxi drivers or in the culture of the City of London. The British no longer lead the world in innovation, but the start-ups of Silicon Roundabout show the spirit of entrepreneurism still lives on. Britain will never be as big as China or Brazil, but we can look forward to a new generation, ready to get to work.

If we are to take advantage of these opportunities, we must get on the side of the responsible, the hard working and the brave. We must stop bailing out the reckless, avoiding all risk, and rewarding laziness.

Compare the actual state of the depressed British to the Brazilians. Yes, Brazil just passed Britain in total wealth, but that is because its population remains three times as big. Britain remains a much safer country, a much richer country and a much more equal country. Britain remains perfectly positioned to take advantage of a future economy where value lies in intellectual capital and being the originators of ideas rather than industrial specialisation. It retains close ties with countries all over the world. London is already the hub of the globalised world. The world speaks its language. For its size, no other nation is more culturally influential in music or literature. It retains enough independence from Europe to not get dragged down by a broken single currency, or an out-of-date social democratic model. Its political system is famously flexible, allowing it to reverse course and correct mistakes far faster than the gridlock of the US Congress. Its democratic culture remains non-corrupt. A ferocious free press ensures one of the largest selection of daily newspapers in the world. Its private schools and leading universities are among the world's best, while its state schools are being reformed rapidly. Unlike Japan or Germany, its demographics are relatively favourable. It remains a young nation. By 2050, it is projected to be the largest country in Europe.

British incomes have doubled in real terms in the last 40 years, but if we work hard there is no reason they could not double again in the next 40. Yes, Britain currently faces very real problems, but they could be overcome. There is much to be optimistic about.

Conclusion

In November 2011 the population of the world reached 7 billion for the first time in human history. In 1950, the population had been little more than 2.5 billion. These bald statistics disguise the immense transformation which has taken place in the world in the last 60 years. New giant economies, like China, India and Brazil, have emerged to rival the traditional dominance of countries in the Western world.

The success of these economies in emerging to prominence contrasts sharply with the economic performance of Britain in the last few years. Britain faced a double-dip recession for the first time since 1975 in the beginning of 2012. It seemed that Europe and Britain in particular were missing out on the growth seen in other parts of the world. Yet the nature of the global economy and competition should offer Europe and Britain opportunities, unparalleled in recent history. It was clear, as 2012 progressed, that Britain should look beyond the confines of Europe to learn how to exploit those opportunities.

Smaller economies like Singapore, Hong Kong and South Korea have shown themselves adept at exploiting the opportunities proffered by global economic growth. In these countries, a combination of private enterprise and effective government policy has enabled economic growth rates which we can only dream about in the West. In China itself, although the political system remains in the grip of the Communist Party, a spirit of enterprise has been prominent in driving economic growth to levels which are scarcely equalled in world history.

Many of these facts are extremely well known, and much comment has been made about them. As British politicians, we feel that it is particularly helpful to learn from the successes of China and other emerging countries. China's march to prominence has been accompanied by rigorous educational standards and an intense spirit of competition. We recognise that in modern Western societies it is impossible to replicate the conditions which have spurred China's growth. We are conscious, however, that some lessons can be learnt and that, indeed, many of those lessons were familiar to us at an earlier stage of our economic development.

Yet, in the aftermath of the financial crisis, and particularly in the wake of the Eurozone crisis, it is only in Western Europe, and partially in the United States, that the voices of pessimism are most loudly heard. *Britannia Unchained* has attempted to confront this phenomenon of increased pessimism. It has been a consistent assumption of the book that many lessons can be learnt from these rising economies.

Britain's recent past has seen different cycles of optimism and pessimism. The immediate postwar years, know as a period of austerity, gave way in the 1950s to an era of rising prosperity. In 1959, Harold Macmillan famously said 'You have never had it so good.' The growing consumerism of that era, however, masked greater uncertainties – decolonisation, the retreat of Empire, happened very quickly. Harold Macmillan, in another of his widely quoted phrases, spoke of 'the winds of change' blowing across the African continent.

The 1960s, especially in London, have been viewed as an era of excitement and innovation. Reducing the voting age from 21 to 18 in 1968, the Beatles, and colour television – all marked an era in which popular culture rose to a dominant place in national life. There was a wider permissiveness in society, and a lot of people, especially younger voters, looked to the future with optimism. The Prime Minister, Harold Wilson, spoke, without any irony, about the 'white heat of technology'. Fashion icons like Twiggy, Jean Shrimpton and Mary Quant became prominent national figures.

By contrast, the 1970s were an era of industrial strife and conflict. The three-day week, miners' strikes and the 'Winter of Discontent' seemed to characterise that era. All through the decade there were rumblings that Britain had become 'ungovernable'. Edward Heath, the Conservative Prime Minister, actually called a general election and framed the question 'Who governs Britain?' He discovered, to his cost, that he and his Government did not. Public spending and inflation continued to run out of control. In 1976 Britain had the humiliation of having to go to the International Monetary Fund. James Callaghan, the increasingly beleaguered Prime Minister, looked out of his depth. Despite his personal popularity, Callaghan lost to the Conservative leader, Margaret Thatcher, in the 1979 general election.

The 1980s saw Margaret Thatcher in her pomp. She openly prided herself on reversing national decline, yet the miners' strike from 1983 to 1984, and the poll tax riots in 1990, perhaps showed how little had changed. The early 1990s saw a recession, and it was only in the middle of that decade that optimism returned to Britain. After leaving the Exchange Rate Mechanism, the British economy expanded and the Labour Party was brought to power under a charismatic leader, Tony Blair. 'Cool Britannia', pop music and open emotionalism were in. More traditional British virtues like restraint and understatement were out.

It was in these Labour years that public spending grew increasingly lavish. The City of London was booming, property prices soared and an over-confident Chancellor of the Exchequer told the nation that there would be no more 'boom and bust'. It seemed like the good years would never end. Personal borrowing increased even more spectacularly than Government spending. Britain's prosperity seemed to be an ever-lasting phenomenon.

The boom of celebrity culture, reality TV, and binge drinking marked an era of indulgence and hedonism. Peter Mandelson openly said that he didn't mind if people became 'filthy rich'. The excesses of that era were unmatched by any in recent British history. Yet it was in this decade that Britain began to slip educationally. Academic attainments, as measured by the PISA tables, began to decline. The vital subjects like science, mathematics and computing that were leading the rest of the world to technological breakthrough were declining in British schools. Despite better grades achieved in schools, there was always the suspicion that standards were falling, and that 'grade inflation' had undermined the value of academic qualifications. The increased wealth of the country masked some worrying trends.

Of course, this prosperity was shown to be based on fickle foundations. By contrast, the emerging economies, like Brazil, India and China, achieved real productivity gains. Their wealth was more securely based on rising exports and a higher degree of academic performance. Their gains were real, while many of ours were illusory. Today, Britons face an unprecedented degree of public and private debt. Once more the question of national decline is being considered. While pessimism is still uncommon, there is a wide degree of uncertainty.

We don't believe that 'decline' is inevitable. The reduction of global poverty and the emergence of new middle classes with commensurate spending power, across Asia and Africa, is a development much to be welcomed. We believe that such a world expanding in so dramatic a fashion offers considerable opportunities for Britain. If Britain is to exploit these opportunities it has to abandon the quick fix and instead put in the fundamental graft, risk and effort that bring long-term rewards.

Notes

Introduction

1. http://www.bbc.co.uk/news/uk-england-london-17380072
2. http://www.nst.com.my/opinion/letters-to-the-editor/two-different-faces-of-the-london-riots-1.58763
3. http://www.nst.com.my/opinion/letters-to-the-editor/two-different-faces-of-the-london-riots-1.58763
4. http://www.bbc.co.uk/news/uk-17261508
5. http://www.dailymail.co.uk/news/article-2024980/London-riots-Ashraf-Rossli-mugged-Malaysian-student-thinks-UK-great.html

Chapter 1

1. http://www.economist.com/node/13315108
2. http://www.economist.com/node/13315108
3. http://www.economist.com/node/13315108
4. Nicholas Crafts, *British Relative Economic Decline Revisited* (2011).
5. Nicholas Crafts, 'British Relative Economic Decline Revisited', Presentation, 2011.
6. Dominic Sandbrook, *State of Emergency* (2010), p. 57.
7. http://news.bbc.co.uk/1/hi/uk_politics/693309.stm
8. Sandbrook, *State of Emergency*, p. 127.
9. Sandbrook, *State of Emergency*, p. 81.
10. http://online.wsj.com/article/SB10001424052748704107104574570122315830890.html
11. http://www.telegraph.co.uk/comment/personal-view/5979462/The-rumours-of-Britains-death-have-been-greatly-exaggerated.html
12. Sandbrook, *State of Emergency*, p. 592.
13. Sandbrook, *State of Emergency*, p. 593.
14. Sandbrook, *State of Emergency*, p. 592.
15. Matt Ridley, *The Rational Optimist* (Fourth Estate, 2010), p. 303.
16. Sandbrook, *State of Emergency*, p. 298.
17. Ridley, *The Rational Optimist*, p. 301.
18. Ridley, *The Rational Optimist*, p. 301.
19. http://www.ejsd.org/public/journal_article/10
20. Crafts, 'British Relative Economic Decline Revisited', Presentation.
21. http://www.thedailybeast.com/newsweek/2009/07/31/forget-the-great-in-britain.html

22. Tim Jackson, *Prosperity without Growth: Economics for a Finite Planet* (2009).
23. nef, *21 Hours* (2010).
24. http://www2.lse.ac.uk/newsAndMedia/news/archives/2005/LSE_SuttonTrust_report.aspx

Chapter 2

1. Wolfram Alpha calculation.
2. David Henderson, *Canada's Budget Triumph* (Mercatus Center, George Mason University, 2010), p. 9.
3. http://www.nytimes.com/learning/general/onthisday/bday/1018.html
4. http://biographi.ca/009004-119.01-e.php?id_nbr=8418
5. Henderson, *Canada's Budget Triumph*, p. 2.
6. Timothy Lewis, *In the Long Run We're All Dead: The Canadian Turn to Fiscal Restraint* (UBC Press, 2003), p. 67.
7. Jocelyn Bourgon, *Program Review: The Government of Canada's Experience Eliminating the Deficit, 1994–99: A Canadian Case Study* (Institute for Government, 2009), p. 11.
8. CentreForum, *Dealing with Debt: Lessons from Abroad* (2010), p. 19.
9. Henderson, *Canada's Budget Triumph*, p. 3.
10. Henderson, *Canada's Budget Triumph*, p. 4.
11. http://reviewcanada.ca/essays/2009/03/01/anyone-for-deficits/
12. Niels Veldhuis, Jason Clemens and Milagros Palacios, *Budget Blueprint: How Lessons from Canada's 1995 Budget Can Be Applied Today* (Fraser Institute, 2011), p. 13.
13. http://www.windsorscottish.com/pl-scp-kcampbell.php
14. Bourgon, *Program Review*, p. 16.
15. Lewis, *In the Long Run We're All Dead*, p. 148.
16. Henderson, *Canada's Budget Triumph*, p. 4.
17. Henderson, *Canada's Budget Triumph*, p. 13.
18. Veldhuis et al., *Budget Blueprint*, p. 20.
19. http://marginalrevolution.com/marginalrevolution/2010/04/the-public-choice-of-spending-cuts.html
20. Andrew Lilico, Ed Holmes and Hiba Sameen, *Controlling Spending and Government Deficits* (Policy Exchange, 2009), p. 80.
21. Henderson, *Canada's Budget Triumph*, p. 13.
22. http://www.independent.co.uk/news/uk/politics/david-cameron-thinks-that-canada-can-show-us-how-to-slash-public-debt-is-he-right-1741920.html
23. (Lilico, et al., *Controlling Spending and Government Deficits*2009), pg p. 80.
24. Henderson, *Canada's Budget Triumph*, p. 8.
25. Henderson, *Canada's Budget Triumph*, p. 17.
26. Henderson, *Canada's Budget Triumph*.
27. http://www.bbc.co.uk/blogs/thereporters/stephanieflanders/2009/03/the_best_prepared_awar.html

28. Thomas Macaulay, *History of England from the Accession of James II* (1848).
29. Macaulay, *History of England*.
30. http://krugman.blogs.nytimes.com/2011/12/04/british-debt-history/
31. http://krugman.blogs.nytimes.com/2011/11/30/bleeding-britain/
32. http://johannhari.com/2011/03/29/the-biggest-lie-in-british-politics/
33. http://www.ft.com/cms/s/0/a9042452-1a3c-11de-9f91-0000779fd2ac. html#axzz1gJPBneNS
34. http://www.newstatesman.com/blogs/david-blanchflower/2011/06/credit-card-cameron-basic
35. Niall Ferguson, *The Cash Nexus: Money and Power in the Modern World, 1700–2000* (Penguin, 2001), p. 53.
36. Ferguson, *The Cash Nexus*, p. 129.
37. Ferguson, *The Cash Nexus*, p. 130.
38. Office for Budget Responsibility, *Economic and Fiscal Outlook*, March 2012.
39. Carmen Reinhart and Kenneth Rogoff, *This Time is Different: Eight Centuries of Financial Folly* (Princeton University Press, 2009).
40. Reinhart and Rogoff, *This Time is Different*.
41. http://www.thedailybeast.com/newsweek/2009/11/27/an-empire-at-risk.html
42. http://www.thedailybeast.com/newsweek/2009/11/27/an-empire-at-risk.html
43. Christina Romer, 'Macroeconomic Policy in the 1960s: The Causes and Consequences of a Mistaken Revolution', Lecture, Economic History Association Annual Meeting, 2007, p. 26.
44. http://voxeu.org/index.php?q=node/5395
45. Manmohan Kumar and Jaejoon Woo, *Public Debt and Growth*, IMF Working Paper (2010).
46. Reinhart and Rogoff, *This Time is Different*, p. xxxii.
47. Edward Nelson and Kalin Nikolov, *UK Inflation in the 1970s and 1980s: The Role of Output Gap Mismeasurement* (Bank of England, 2001), p. 14.
48. Romer, 'Macroeconomic Policy in the 1960s', p. 9.
49. http://news.bbc.co.uk/1/hi/uk_politics/3288907.stm
50. Edward Balls, *Euro-Monetarism: How Britain was Ensnared and How it Should Escape* (Fabian Society, 1992).
51. http://blogs.independent.co.uk/2011/03/30/origins-of-the-cameron-balls-feud/
52. http://www.economist.com/node/105528
53. http://blogs.independent.co.uk/2011/03/30/origins-of-the-cameron-balls-feud/
54. At the time, Permanent Secretary for the Treasury.
55. HM Treasury, *Reforming Britain's Economic and Financial Policy: Towards Greater Economic Stability* (Palgrave, 2002), p. 1.
56. HM Treasury, *Reforming Britain's Economic and Financial Policy*, p. xi.
57. Robert Peston, *Brown's Britain* (Short Books, 2006), p. 167.
58. Peston, *Brown's Britain*, p. 42.
59. William Keegan, *The Prudence of Mr Brown* (Wiley, 2003), p. 250.

60. Keegan, *The Prudence of Mr Brown*, 2003.
61. http://www.independent.co.uk/opinion/profile-ed-balls--browns-young-egghead-1148933.html
62. Peston, *Brown's Britain*, p. 171.
63. Peston, *Brown's Britain*, p. 174.
64. http://specials.ft.com/budget2002/FT3QIZPK50D.html
65. Peston, *Brown's Britain*, p. 273.
66. http://budgetresponsibility.independent.gov.uk/pubs/Historical-Budget-forecastsFER2011.xls
67. http://specials.ft.com/budget2002/FT3NMVSU60D.html
68. A structural surplus or deficit is the estimated budget balance ignoring temporary effects from a boom or bust. Structural balance ensures a balanced budget in the medium term, without any discretionary decisions on the Government's part.
69. http://www.nber.org/digest/nov11/w17239.html
70. HM Treasury, *Reforming Britain's Economic and Financial Policy*, p. 354.
71. http://www.independent.co.uk/money/loans-credit/for-the-first-time-britons-personal-debt-exceeds-britains-gdp-462825.html
72. http://www.guardian.co.uk/money/2007/aug/02/business.creditanddebt
73. http://news.bbc.co.uk/1/hi/uk/8608935.stm
74. http://www8.open.ac.uk/platform/blogs/society-matters/household-debt-reaches-unprecedented-levels
75. http://www.bbc.co.uk/news/business-15820601
76. McKinsey Global Institute, *Debt and Deleveraging: Uneven Progress on the Path to Growth* (2012).
77. http://www.guardian.co.uk/politics/2003/may/07/labour.politicalcolumnists
78. http://www.guardian.co.uk/media/1999/dec/22/bbc.futureofthenhs
79. http://www.guardian.co.uk/politics/2000/mar/17/comment.pollytoynbee
80. http://www.guardian.co.uk/society/2001/mar/08/3
81. http://www.guardian.co.uk/society/2001/nov/23/comment
82. http://blogs.ft.com/money-supply/2011/11/30/the-uk-hangover-gets-worse/#axzz1h5FjxNF3
83. http://www.economist.com/node/18719530
84. International Monetary Fund, World Economic Outlook Database (April 2011).
85. http://www.economist.com/node/18719530
86. http://www.imf.org/external/np/ms/2009/030909a.htm
87. http://www.economist.com/node/16060113
88. Michael Bordo, Angela Redish and Hugh Rockoff, *Why Didn't Canada Have a Banking Crisis in 2008 (or in 1930, or in 1907, or in 1983)* (2010).
89. http://www.economist.com/node/16060113
90. http://www.ft.com/cms/s/0/db2b340a-0a1b-11df-8b23-00144feabdc0.html#axzz1oEUdacsd
91. http://www.ft.com/cms/s/0/75b43310-ebee-11de-930c-00144feab49a.html#axzz1nrHw5tUL
92. Heritage Foundation, *Index of Economic Freedom* (2011).

93. Cato Institute, *Economic Freedom of the World* (2011).
94. http://www.oecd.org/dataoecd/54/12/46643496.pdf

Chapter 3

1. http://www.theatlantic.com/magazine/archive/2011/07/the-world-8217-s-schoolmaster/8532/2/
2. http://www.theatlantic.com/magazine/archive/2011/07/the-world-8217-s-schoolmaster/8532/2/
3. http://www.goethe.de/wis/fut/dos/gdw/sla/en2528036.htm
4. http://www.aicgs.org/publication/why-is-there-no-pisa-shock-in-the-u-s-a-comparison-of-german-and-american-education-policy/
5. http://www2.ed.gov/pubs/NatAtRisk/risk.html
6. http://voices.washingtonpost.com/answer-sheet/school-turnaroundsreform/how-ronald-reagan-affected-tod.html
7. http://www.theatlantic.com/magazine/archive/2011/07/the-world-8217-s-schoolmaster/8532/2/
8. http://www.theatlantic.com/magazine/archive/2011/07/the-world-8217-s-schoolmaster/8532/2/
9. http://www.oecd.org/document/53/0,3746,en_32252351_32235731_38262901_1_1_1_1,00.html
10. http://www.theatlantic.com/magazine/archive/2011/07/the-world-8217-s-schoolmaster/8532/2/
11. http://www.nytimes.com/2003/02/07/news/07iht-schools_ed3_.html?pagewanted=all
12. http://www.nytimes.com/2003/02/07/news/07iht-schools_ed3_.html?pagewanted=all
13. http://www.aicgs.org/publication/why-is-there-no-pisa-shock-in-the-u-s-a-comparison-of-german-and-american-education-policy/
14. http://www.theatlantic.com/magazine/archive/2011/07/the-world-8217-s-schoolmaster/8532/2/
15. http://www.pearsonfoundation.org/oecd/germany.html
16. http://www.pearsonfoundation.org/oecd/germany.html
17. http://www.german-times.com/index.php?option=com_content&task=view&id=3205&Itemid=81
18. http://www.tes.co.uk/article.aspx?storycode=6065634
19. http://www.nytimes.com/2011/11/06/education/edlife/why-science-majors-change-their-mind-its-just-so-darn-hard.html?pagewanted=all
20. http://online.wsj.com/article/SB10001424052970203733504577026212798573518.html?mod=WSJ_Careers_CareerJournal_2
21. http://www.cbsnews.com/8301-505145_162-37241878/5-hardest-and-easiest-college-majors-by-gpas/?tag=mwuser
22. http://www.agr.org.uk/Content/draft80; http://www.guardian.co.uk/education/mortarboard/2011/feb/07/career-advice-a-levels

23. Jeremy Hodgen, David Pepper, Linda Sturman and Graham Ruddock, *Is the UK an Outlier?* (Nuffield Foundation, 2010).
24. http://www.ofqual.gov.uk/files/QCA_3388_Maths_GCE_eval_report.pdf
25. http://news.bbc.co.uk/1/hi/uk/665308.stm
26. http://www.tes.co.uk/article.aspx?storycode=2357606
27. Laura Kounine, John Marks and Elizabeth Truss, *The Value of Mathematics* (Reform, 2008).
28. Taxpayers' Alliance, *The Non-Courses Book* (2007).
29. Survey for the Centre for Higher Education Research and Information, 2009, reported in the *Sunday Times*, 2 September 2010.
30. http://news.lenovo.com/article_display.cfm?article_id=1532
31. http://www.economist.com/node/21542222
32. http://www.economist.com/node/21542222
33. http://www.economist.com/node/21541713
34. T. Friedman and M. Mandelbaum, *That Used to Be Us: How America Fell Behind in the World it Invented and How we can Come Back* (Little, Brown, 2011).
35. http://www.jwobrien.com/China_MFE_F1.pdf
36. http://www.bbc.co.uk/news/10506798
37. http://faststream.civilservice.gov.uk/
38. Kounine et al., *The Value of Mathematics*.
39. http://www.gresham.ac.uk/lectures-and-events/how-do-we-deal-with-rewards-for-failure-while-supporting-growth
40. Kounine et al., *The Value of Mathematics*.
41. http://www.thetimes.co.uk/tto/opinion/columnists/anushkaasthana/article3215880.ece
42. http://www.washingtonpost.com/wp-srv/politics/documents/Obama_Economy_Georgetown.html;
43. A. Saini, *Geek Nation: How Indian Science is Taking Over the World* (Hodder and Stoughton,2011); http://www.forbes.com/sites/ciocentral/2011/01/20/danger-america-is-losing-its-edge-in-innovation/
44. http://www.prlog.org/10536256-over-half-of-young-people-want-to-be-famous.html
45. http://www.taylorherring.com/blog/index.php/tag/traditional-careers/
46. http://www.global-science.net/images2/10-Facts-Fictions.pdf
47. http://www.taylorherring.com/blog/index.php/tag/traditional-careers/
48. http://www.guardian.co.uk/news/datablog/2011/jun/15/a-level-subjects-preferred-by-universities-by-private-school-and-comprehensive
49. http://eprints.lse.ac.uk/33550/1/sercdp0056.pdf
50. http://eprints.lse.ac.uk/33550/1/sercdp0056.pdf
51. http://math.bu.edu/people/murad/MarkWhitehouseSlicesofRisk.txt
52. http://clubs.ntu.edu.sg/rms/resources/research_modeling.pdf
53. http://math.bu.edu/people/murad/MarkWhitehouseSlicesofRisk.txt
54. http://clubs.ntu.edu.sg/rms/resources/research_modeling.pdf
55. http://www.wired.com/techbiz/it/magazine/17-03/wp_quant?currentPage=all

56. http://www.ft.com/cms/s/0/912d85e8-2d75-11de-9eba-00144feabdc0.
html#axzz1jiu5N1Eg

57. http://www.thetimes.co.uk/tto/life/article3252170.ece; http://www.
thesundaytimes.co.uk/sto/style/living/article149456.ece

58. http://geekout.blogs.cnn.com/

59. http://www.huffingtonpost.com/2011/07/06/google-marissa-mayer-women-
in-tech_n_891167.html?ref=women-in-tech

60. http://www.nytimes.com/2007/04/17/science/17comp.html?_r=2&8dpc=&
oref=slogin&pagewanted=all&oref=slogin

61. http://healthland.time.com/2011/08/18/study-are-women-choosing-
romance-over-math-and-science/

62. http://eco.cueb.edu.cn/contents/page/html.php?id=20110811051315AAc6vyM

63. Engineering UK, *Engineering UK 2012: The State of Engineering*, http://
www.engineeringuk.com/what_we_do/education_&_skills/engineering_
uk_12.cfm; http://ncwit.org/pdf/ByTheNumbers09.pdf; http://www.ft.com/
cms/s/0/12623ca4-a636-11e0-8eef-00144feabdc0.html#axzz1iOBsL3Mw

64. http://www.bloomberg.com/news/2011-08-03/higher-pay-not-luring-u-s-
women-to-technical-jobs-study-finds.html

65. http://www.forbes.com/sites/ciocentral/2011/01/20/danger-america-is-losing-
its-edge-in-innovation/

66. Saini, *Geek Nation*.

67. http://boss.blogs.nytimes.com/2011/06/24/why-women-have-an-advantage-
in-technology/

68. http://www.economist.com/node/13496638

69. http://machinedesign.com/article/engineering-in-india-1108; http://www.
economist.com/blogs/dailychart/2011/05/poor_economics

70. http://www.ox.ac.uk/about_the_university/facts_and_figures/undergraduate_
admissions_statistics/index.html; http://epaper.timesofindia.com/Repository/
TOIBG/2010/01/16/TOIBG_2010_1_16_20.pdf

71. Saini, *Geek Nation*.

72. http://ibnlive.in.com/news/hyderabad-boy-prudhvi-teja-tops-iitjee/154163-3.
html; http://www.hindu.com/2008/05/31/stories/2008053154271000.htm

73. Saini, *Geek Nation*.

74. http://www.educationindiaworld.com/2010/02/17/iit-jee-topper-nitin-jains-
my-success-story-going-to-publish/

75. http://www.nitinjainiittopper.com/

76. http://news.lenovo.com/article_display.cfm?article_id=1532

77. http://anitaborg.org/files/womenhightechworld.pdf

78. http://news.lenovo.com/article_display.cfm?article_id=1532

79. http://www.techrepublic.com/blog/programming-and-development/it-gender-
gap-where-are-the-female-programmers/2386;

80. http://news.lenovo.com/article_display.cfm?article_id=1532

81. http://epaper.timesofindia.com/Repository/TOIBG/2010/01/16/
TOIBG_2010_1_16_20.pdf; http://machinedesign.com/article/engineering-
in-india-1108

82. http://www.bbc.co.uk/news/business-12597815

83. http://indiatoday.intoday.in/story/lok-sabha-approves-eight-new-iits-and-bhu-it-gets-the-nod/1/133305.html

84. http://www.bbc.co.uk/news/business-12597815

85. http://articles.economictimes.indiatimes.com/2011-12-13/news/30511978_1_growth-projection-growth-forecast-fitch

86. http://www.ukces.org.uk/assets/bispartners/ukces/docs/publications/briefing-paper-the-supply-of-and-demand-for-high-level-stem-skills.pdf

87. http://www.education.gov.uk/rsgateway/DB/SFR/s001055/index.shtml (table 3); http://www.hesa.ac.uk/content/view/1897/239/ (table 2).

88. Hansard HC vol 530 cols 1298W (6 July 2011).

89. http://www.ukces.org.uk/assets/bispartners/ukces/docs/publications/briefing-paper-the-supply-of-and-demand-for-high-level-stem-skills.pdf

90. E.A. Jamison, D.T. Jamison and E.A. Hanushek, 'The Effects of Education Quality on Income Growth and Mortality Decline', *Economics of Education Review*, 6, vol. 26 (2007).

91. R.D. Lansbury, N. Wailes and A. Kirsh, *Globalization, Continuity and Change: The Automotive Assembly Industry* (2008).

92. A. Marshall, *Industry and Trade* (1919).

93. http://www.timeshighereducation.co.uk/world-university-rankings/2011-2012/top-400.html

94. http://www.guardian.co.uk/education/2011/may/31/universities-world-class-rankings

95. http://www.timeshighereducation.co.uk/story.asp?sectioncode=26&storycode=417364&c=1

96. House of Lords Science and Technology Sub-Committee, 'Call for Evidence: Higher Education in STEM Subjects', Submission by the Council for the Mathematical Sciences (15 December 2011).

97. http://articles.timesofindia.indiatimes.com/2011-03-29/chennai/29357309_1_iit-m-m-s-ananth-iit-madras

98. Royal Society, *Knowledge, Networks and Nations: Global Scientific Colloboration in the 21st Century* (2011).

99. D. Autor, *The Polarization of Job Opportunities in the U.S. Labor Market: Implications for Employment and Earnings* (Center for American Progress and the Hamilton Project, 2010).

100. Ian Brinkley, *Manufacturing and the Knowledge Economy* (The Work Foundation, 2009).

101. Elizabeth Truss, *Academic Rigour and Social Mobility: How Low Income Students are being Kept Out of Top Jobs* (CentreForum, 2011).

102. Jonathan Adams and James Wilsdon, *The New Geography of Science: UK Research and International Colloboration* (Demos, 2006).

103. Royal Society, *Knowledge, Networks and Nations.*

104. Royal Society, *Knowledge, Networks and Nations.*

105. http://www.nytimes.com/2012/01/22/business/apple-america-and-a-squeezed-middle-class.html?pagewanted=all

106. E.A. Hanushek and L. Woessmann, 'The Role of Cognitive Skills in Economic Development', *Journal of Economic Literature*, 3, vol. 46 (2008).

107. Hanushek and Woessmann, 'The Role of Cognitive Skills in Economic Development'.
108. Hanushek and Woessmann, 'The Role of Cognitive Skills in Economic Development'.
109. Hanushek and Woessmann, 'The Role of Cognitive Skills in Economic Development'.
110. Hanushek and Woessmann, 'The Role of Cognitive Skills in Economic Development'.
111. L. Pritchett, 'Does Learning to Add Up Add Up? The Returns to Schooling in Aggregate Data', *Handbook of the Economics of Education* (2006); Jamison et al., 'The Effects of Education Quality'.
112. *Digital Technology: A Review of Intellectual Property and Growth*, an independent report by Prof. Ian Hargreaves (May 2011), pp. 12–14.
113. http://www.deloitte.com/view/en_GB/uk/industries/tmt/b9c589a865f05310 VgnVCM2000001b56f00aRCRD.htm
114. http://consumers.ofcom.org.uk/2011/08/a-nation-addicted-to-smartphones/
115. http://www.guardian.co.uk/business/2011/nov/27/tech-city-digital-startups-shoreditch
116. http://www.oecd.org/officialdocuments/publicdisplaydocumentpdf/?cote= ECO/WKP(2011)57&docLanguage=En
117. http://www.oecd.org/officialdocuments/publicdisplaydocumentpdf/?cote =ECO/WKP(2011)57&docLanguage=En; http://www.washingtontimes. com/news/2011/dec/13/more-school-hours-dont-guarantee-better-test-score/?page=all
118. Harris Interactive, 'STEM Perceptions: Student & Parent Study – Parents and Students Weigh In on How to Inspire the Next Generation of Doctors, Scientists, Software Developers and Engineers', 2011, http://www.microsoft. com/en-us/news/presskits/citizenship/docs/STEMPerceptionsReport.pdf
119. http://www.bbc.co.uk/news/education-14823042; http://www.telegraph. co.uk/education/educationnews/9037571/Universities-dropping-science-in-favour-of-media-studies.html
120. http://www.futuremorph.org/scienceandmaths/#/intro
121. Rob Eastaway, *Why Parents Can't Do Maths Today*, http://www.bbc.co.uk/ news/magazine-11258175 (2010).
122. http://www.thetimes.co.uk/tto/opinion/columnists/article3272610.ece
123. Tom Sastry and Bahram Bekhradnia, 'The Academic Experience of Students in English Universities', 2007, http://www.hepi.ac.uk/466-1309/The-Academic-Experience-of-Students-in-English-Universities-(2007-report).html
124. June 2007.
125. http://www.nickbolesmp.com/downloads/macmillan-lecture-tory-reform-group-30th-january-2012.pdf
126. http://www.thetimes.co.uk/tto/opinion/columnists/article3272610.ece
127. http://www.thetimes.co.uk/tto/business/moversshakers/article3273435.ece
128. http://www.thetimes.co.uk/tto/business/moversshakers/article3273435.ece
129. http://www.bis.gov.uk/news/speeches/david-willetts-policy-exchange-britain-best-place-science-2012

130. http://www.londonpressservice.org.uk/lps/tradeindustry/item/243100.html
131. http://www.timeshighereducation.co.uk/story.asp?storycode=418739
132. *Guardian*, 23 January 2012.
133. http://www.ft.com/cms/s/0/9466007a-c970-11e0-9eb8-00144feabdc0.html#axzz1krKKMx3Q
134. http://www.ucas.com/about_us/media_enquiries/media_releases/ 2012/20120130
135. http://www.nytimes.com/2011/06/11/technology/11computing.html?pagewanted=1&_r=1

Chapter 4

1. RSA, *Inside the Mind of a Cabbie* (2011).
2. http://www.thisismoney.co.uk/money/article-1690284/How-I-turned-taxis-into-a-170m-business.html
3. http://www.guardian.co.uk/business/2009/dec/20/addison-lee-john-griffin-profile
4. http://www.moneyweek.com/news-and-charts/profile-of-entrepreneur-john-griffin-of-addison-lee-48133
5. http://www.moneyweek.com/news-and-charts/profile-of-entrepreneur-john-griffin-of-addison-lee-48133
6. *Evening Standard*, 25 February 2009.
7. http://www.londonlovesbusiness.com/addison-lee-founder-john-griffin-on-building-his-200m-minicab-empire/1787.article
8. http://www.bbc.co.uk/news/health-16086233
9. http://www.guardian.co.uk/uk/2011/oct/03/tube-drivers-salaries-50000
10. 'The Poles are Coming', BBC2, 11 March 2008.
11. *Evening Standard*, 9 October 2007.
12. *Daily Telegraph*, 21 May 2011.
13. S. Lee, D. McCann and J. Messenger, *Working Time Around the World* (Routledge, 2007).
14. Data available online from the Conference Board, http://www.conference-board.org/data/economydatabase/.
15. OECD, *Society at a Glance* (2011).
16. Niall Ferguson, *Civilization* (2011).
17. http://www.guardian.co.uk/world/2010/oct/18/french-strikers-cause-stink-marseille
18. Conference Board, http://www.conference-board.org/data/economydatabase/.
19. World Bank, Labour participation rate.
20. ONS, *Labour Market Statistics*, January 2012.
21. ONS, *International Comparisons of Productivity – 2010 – Final Estimates* (2012).
22. ONS, *International Comparisons of Productivity*.
23. M. Phelps, *Total Public Service Output and Productivity* (UK Centre for the Measurement of Government Activity, Office for National Statistics, 2009).

24. Centre for Social Justice, *Breakdown Britain* (2006); Centre for Social Justice, *Breakthrough Britain* (2007).
25. David Willetts, *The Pinch: How the Baby Boomers Took Their Children's Future – And Why They Should Give it Back* (Atlantic Books, 2010).
26. http://it.tmcnet.com/topics/it/articles/147893-intel-build-advanced-semiconductor-fab-arizona.htm
27. http://www.theregister.co.uk/2011/02/01/arm_holdings_q4_2010_numbers/
28. Edward Prescott and W.P. Cary, 'Why do Americans Work so Much More than Europeans?', *Federal Reserve Bank of Minneapolis Quarterly Review* (2004).
29. Steven Davis and Magnus Henrekson, *Tax Effects on Work Activity* (2004).
30. HM Treasury, Public finances databank; ONS, Labour Force Survey, 8 December 2011.
31. HMRC, *Income Tax Liabilities, by Income Range*, http://www.hmrc.gov.uk/stats/income_tax/menu.htm
32. Alberto Alesina, Edward Glaeser and Bruce Sacerdote, *Work and Leisure in the US and Europe: Why so Different?* (2005).
33. http://scrapthetax.co.uk/newsshow.aspx?id=3
34. ONS, *Labour Market Statistics* and *Economics and Labour Market Review* The data for 2011 cover January to November inclusive.
35. Data from the Department of Work and Pensions, May 2011.
36. Jean-Baptiste Michau, *European Unemployment: How Significant was a Declining Work Ethic* (CentrePiece, 2009).
37. Various ONS data.
38. Department of Work and Pensions, Press Release, 25 January 2012.
39. YouGov poll commissioned by the Centre for Social Justice, May 2008.
40. Centre for Social Justice, *Dynamic Benefits: Towards Welfare That Works. A Policy Report by the CSJ Economic Dependency Working Group* (2009), p. 7.
41. OECD, *Family Database,* 2011.
42. Elizabeth Truss, 'Why We Need Better Policies for Working Parents'. Article for the Institute of Directors, 2011.
43. Published 7 September 2011.
44. Interview, *Daily Mail*, 19 September 2009.
45. Interview, *Guardian*, 7 February 2011.
46. Centre for Social Justice, *Creating Opportunity, Rewarding Ambition* (2011).
47. CBI, *Action for Jobs* (2011).
48. Andrew Dunn, 'The "Dole or Drudgery" Dilemma', *Social Policy & Administration*, 1, vol. 44 (2010).
49. http://www.bbc.co.uk/news/uk-england-birmingham-16037332
50. http://www.dailymail.co.uk/news/article-2085142/Cait-Reilly-Unemployed-graduate-sues-ministers-forced-work-Poundland.html#ixzz1odGVxdHi
51. Widely reported, including *Daily Telegraph*, 1 October 2009.
52. *Daily Telegraph*, 10 October 2009.
53. Interview, *Guardian*, 10 December 2011.
54. Alan Sugar, *The Way I See It* (2011), pp. 145–6.

55. Reported, *Digital Spy*, 18 October 2011.

56. http://news.bbc.co.uk/1/hi/business/6923678.stm

57. http://www.telegraph.co.uk/culture/books/biographyandmemoirreviews/8081734/Alan-Sugar-the-Essex-boy-who-showed-em-all.html

58. http://www.thisismoney.co.uk/money/article-1711658/How-rich-Alan-Sugar.html

59. Jo Blanden and Stephen Machin, *Recent Changes in Intergenerational Mobility in Britain* (Centre for Economic Performance, 2007); Panel on Fair Access to the Professions, *Unleashing Aspiration* (2009).

60. OECD, *A Family Affair: Intergenerational Social Mobility Across OECD Countries* (2010).

Chapter 5

1. Bernard Bar-Natan, 2012 interview (email).

2. Bar-Natan, 2012 interview.

3. http://www.jpost.com/Opinion/Columnists/Article.aspx?id=218376

4. Bar-Natan, 2012 interview.

5. Bar-Natan, 2012 interview.

6. Jonah Lehrer, *Imagine: How Creativity Works* (2012).

7. http://www.economist.com/node/10881264?story_id=10881264

8. http://www.mbs.edu/home/defontenay/IsraelSiliconWadiJune2002.pdf

9. http://english.themarker.com/israel-s-economic-growth-in-2010-bests-forecasts-1.334167

10. http://www.reuters.com/article/2011/12/15/us-apple-israel-rd-id USTRE7BE0KT20111215

11. http://www.jlaw.com/Commentary/SupremeChutzpah.html

12. http://www.mbs.edu/home/defontenay/IsraelSiliconWadiJune2002.pdf

13. http://www.forbes.com/sites/danisenberg/2011/02/11/start-up-notions-where-israeli-entrepreneurship-really-came-from/

14. http://www.city-journal.org/2009/19_3_jewish-capitalism.html

15. Bar-Natan 2012 interview.

16. Meaning 'initiative' in Hebrew.

17. http://ideas.economist.com/blog/seeding-entrepreneurship

18. http://www.telegraph.co.uk/news/9050088/Solar-panels-subsidy-was-one-of-the-most-ridiculous-schemes-ever-dreamed-up-Lord-Marland-says.html

19. http://www.city-journal.org/2009/19_3_jewish-capitalism.html

20. http://www.telegraph.co.uk/technology/news/8652076/Israel-The-start-up-nation-taking-on-Silicon-Valley.html

21. http://www.spiked-online.com/index.php/site/article/9768/

22. http://www.bbc.co.uk/news/business-11652824

23. Dominic Raab, *Escaping the Strait Jacket* (2011).

24. World Economic Forum, *Global Competitiveness Report 2011/12* (2012), p. 515.

25. http://www.wired.com/magazine/2011/12/mf_neuwirth_qa/all/1

26. Robert Neuwirth, *Stealth of Nations: The Global Rise of the Informal Economy* (Pantheon Books, 2011).
27. http://www.wired.com/magazine/2011/12/mf_neuwirth_qa/all/1
28. http://nwo.li.com/book/index.html
29. Niall Ferguson, *The Ascent of Money: A Financial History of the World* (2008).
30. http://www.thisislondon.co.uk/lifestyle/london-life/sir-jonathan-ive-the-iman-cometh-7562170.html
31. Tim Harford, *Adapt: Why Success Always Starts with Failure* (2011).
32. http://www.economist.com/node/18557776
33. Private email.
34. Robert Fairlee and Aaron Chatterji, *High Technology Entrepreneurship in Silicon Valley* (2011).
35. http://online.wsj.com/article/SB10001424052970204624204577179193752435590.html
36. Fairlee and Chatterji, *High Technology Entrepreneurship.*
37. BVCA, *Benchmarking UK Venture Capital to the US and Israel: What Lessons can be Learned?* (2009).
38. World Economic Forum, *Global Competitiveness Report 2011/12*, p. 484.
39. http://www.time.com/time/magazine/article/0,9171,2099675,00.html
40. http://www.time.com/time/magazine/article/0,9171,2099675,00.html
41. http://news.bbc.co.uk/1/hi/business/4328341.stm
42. http://online.wsj.com/article/SB115352188346314087.html
43. http://online.wsj.com/article/SB115352188346314087.html
44. http://www.wired.co.uk/news/archive/2012-02/06/silicon-roundabout

Chapter 6

1. http://ironicsurrealism.com/2011/03/20/transcript-obama-speech-rio-de-janeiro-brazil-march-20-2011/
2. http://www.nytimes.com/2011/03/21/world/americas/21brazil.html?pagewanted=all
3. http://www.ipsos-na.com/download/pr.aspx?id=10347
4. http://news.xinhuanet.com/english2010/indepth/2010-10/02/c_13540088.htm
5. http://aiesecubc.wordpress.com/2010/11/14/brazil/
6. http://coa.counciloftheamericas.org/articles/3871/Brazil%E2%80%99s_President:_Dilma_Rousseff%E2%80%99s_First_Year/
7. http://aiesecubc.wordpress.com/2010/11/14/brazil/
8. http://www.bbc.co.uk/news/business-16332115
9. http://www.businessweek.com/bwdaily/dnflash/content/nov2007/db20071115_045316.htm
10. http://www.economist.com/blogs/newsbook/2010/07/brazils_prospects
11. http://www.forbes.com/forbes/2011/0509/global-2000-11-edward-glaeser-slums-dharavi-lands-opportunity_2.html

12. http://www.forbes.com/sites/megacities/2011/04/08/curfew-in-the-favela/
13. http://techcrunch.com/2010/05/12/coming-up-from-the-favelas-brazils-slumdog-entrepreneurs/
14. http://www.guardian.co.uk/world/2011/nov/13/brazil-troops-raid-shantytown
15. http://www.bbc.co.uk/news/world-latin-america-15710719
16. http://www.telegraph.co.uk/news/worldnews/southamerica/brazil/8890151/Rio-plans-to-pacify-dozens-more-favelas.html
17. http://www.bbc.co.uk/worldclass/16705801
18. http://www.forbes.com/sites/megacities/2011/04/19/favela-fashion-overcoming-business-challenges/
19. http://techcrunch.com/2010/05/08/making-lemonade-out-of-bureaucratic-brazilian-lemons/
20. http://techcrunch.com/2010/05/08/making-lemonade-out-of-bureaucratic-brazilian-lemons/
21. http://quererempreender.blogspot.co.uk/2009/03/edivan-fundador-da-sedi.html
22. http://www.forbes.com/sites/julieruvolo/2012/01/23/bye-bye-brazilian-blowouts-the-next-big-brazilian-hair-trend-is-beleza-natural/
23. http://www.endeavor.org/entrepreneurs/leila-velez/97
24. http://www.economist.com/node/21528985
25. http://www.bbc.co.uk/news/business-11477974
26. http://www.economist.com/node/21528985
27. http://www.ft.com/cms/s/0/71352352-112c-11e1-ad22-00144feabdc0.html#axzz1kGsfWbFB
28. http://www.guardian.co.uk/news/datablog/2011/oct/10/world-murder-rate-unodc
29. http://www.economist.com/node/21528985
30. http://www.pisa.oecd.org/dataoecd/54/12/46643496.pdf
31. http://www.reuters.com/article/2011/10/31/us-foxconn-brazil-id USTRE79T17C20111031
32. Paul Krugman, *The Myth of Asia's Miracle* (1994).
33. http://seekingalpha.com/article/262949-is-brazil-a-paper-jaguar
34. http://marginalrevolution.com/marginalrevolution/2011/04/why-do-brazilians-emigrate-so-infrequently.html
35. Frédéric Docquier, B. Lindsay Lowell and Abdeslam Marfouk, *A Gendered Assessment of Highly Skilled Emigration* (2009).
36. http://www.bbc.co.uk/blogs/theeditors/2010/03/brazil_sustained_flight.html
37. http://inventorspot.com/articles/japans_golden_age_seniors_get_smaller_silver_cups_24672
38. http://www.ft.com/cms/s/0/c9ca56b0-806d-11de-bf04-00144feabdc0.html#axzz1otYH5PH9
39. http://ukhousebubble.blogspot.co.uk/2011/10/coming-demographic-crisis-new.html

40. http://www.guardian.co.uk/world/2012/jan/30/japan-population-shrink-third
41. http://www.economist.com/blogs/dailychart/2010/11/japans_population
42. http://www.independent.co.uk/news/world/asia/japan-a-country-in-crisis-413212.html
43. http://www.guardian.co.uk/world/2012/jan/30/japan-population-shrink-third
44. http://www.economist.com/node/18832070
45. http://www.economist.com/node/18832070
46. http://www.economist.com/node/18832070
47. http://www.thelocal.de/society/20091118-23365.html
48. http://english.peopledaily.com.cn/200601/20/eng20060120_236944.html
49. http://www.time.com/time/world/article/0,8599,1991216,00.html
50. http://www.spiegel.de/international/germany/0,1518,779741,00.html
51. http://www.thelocal.de/society/20091118-23365.html
52. http://english.peopledaily.com.cn/200601/20/eng20060120_236944.html
53. http://www.telegraph.co.uk/news/uknews/8634994/Baby-boom-down-to-benefits-delayed-motherhood-and-immigrants-says-ONS.html
54. http://www.telegraph.co.uk/news/uknews/8634994/Baby-boom-down-to-benefits-delayed-motherhood-and-immigrants-says-ONS.html
55. http://www.sustainablegov.co.uk/health/britains-brand-new-baby-boom-why-now-and-how-will-we-cope
56. http://www.guardian.co.uk/education/2012/feb/03/baby-boom-schools-breaking-point
57. http://www.guardian.co.uk/education/2012/feb/03/baby-boom-schools-breaking-point
58. http://www.guardian.co.uk/education/2012/feb/03/baby-boom-schools-breaking-point
59. http://www.telegraph.co.uk/news/uknews/8634994/Baby-boom-down-to-benefits-delayed-motherhood-and-immigrants-says-ONS.html
60. http://www.telegraph.co.uk/news/uknews/8634994/Baby-boom-down-to-benefits-delayed-motherhood-and-immigrants-says-ONS.html
61. http://www.telegraph.co.uk/news/uknews/8634994/Baby-boom-down-to-benefits-delayed-motherhood-and-immigrants-says-ONS.html
62. Max Wind-Cowie and Thomas Gregor, *A Place for Pride* (Demos, 2011).
63. http://www.telegraph.co.uk/property/9123806/After-40-years-why-should-I-be-forced-to-sell-my-property.html
64. David Willetts, *The Pinch: How the Baby Boomers Took Their Children's Future – And Why They Should Give it Back* (Atlantic Books, 2010).
65. http://www.dailymail.co.uk/news/article-2055497/JEREMY-PAXMAN-Baby-Boomers-selfish-generation-history.html
66. http://www.telegraph.co.uk/finance/personalfinance/pensions/8840963/Baby-boomers-are-very-privileged-human-beings.html
67. http://www.telegraph.co.uk/finance/personalfinance/pensions/8840963/Baby-boomers-are-very-privileged-human-beings.html

68. http://www.economist.com/node/15495760
69. http://www.telegraph.co.uk/finance/personalfinance/pensions/8840963/
Baby-boomers-are-very-privileged-human-beings.html
70. http://www.economist.com/node/15495760
71. http://www.ft.com/cms/s/0/7831bd68-6f56-11e1-b368-00144feab49a.
html#axzz1paqUyRCO

Bibliography

Adams, Jonathan, and James Wilsdon, *The New Geography of Science: UK Research and International Colloboration* (Demos, 2006).

Alesina, Alberto, Edward Glaeser and Bruce Sacerdote, *Work and Leisure in the US and Europe: Why So Different?* (2005).

Autor, D., *The Polarization of Job Opportunities in the U.S. Labor Market: Implications for Employment and Earnings* (Center for American Progress and the Hamilton Project, 2010).

Balls, Edward, *Euro-Monetarism: How Britain was Ensnared and How it Should Escape* (Fabian Society, 1992).

Blanden, Jo, and Stephen Machin, *Recent Changes in Intergenerational Mobility in Britain* (Centre for Economic Performance, 2007).

Bordo, Michael D., Angela Redish and Hugh Rockoff, *Why Didn't Canada have a Banking Crisis in 2008 (or in 1930, or in 1907, or in 1983)* (2010).

Bourgon, Jocelyn, *Program Review: The Government of Canada's Experience Eliminating the Deficit, 1994–99: A Canadian Case Study* (Institute for Government, 2009).

Bradshaw, Jenny, et al., *PISA 2009: Achievement of 15-Year-Olds in England* (NFER, 2010).

Brinkley, Ian, *Manufacturing and the Knowledge Economy* (The Work Foundation, 2009).

BVCA, *Benchmarking UK Venture Capital to the US and Israel: What Lessons can be Learned?* (2009).

Cato Institute, *Economic Freedom of the World* (2011).

CBI, *Action for Jobs* (2011).

Centre for Social Justice, *Breakdown Britain* (2006).

Centre for Social Justice, *Breakthrough Britain* (2007).

Centre for Social Justice, *Creating Opportunity, Rewarding Ambition* (2011).

Centre for Social Justice, *Dynamic Benefits: Towards Welfare That Works*. A Policy Report by the CSJ Economic Dependency Working Group (2009).

CentreForum, *Dealing with Debt: Lessons from Abroad* (2010).

Clark, Tom, and Andrew Dilnot, *Measuring the UK Fiscal Stance Since the Second World War* (IFS, 2002).

Crafts, Nicholas, *British Relative Economic Decline Revisited* (2011).

Crafts, Nicholas, 'British Relative Economic Decline Revisited', Presentation, 2011.

Davis, Steven, and Magnus Henrekson, *Tax Effects on Work Activity* (NBER, 2004).

Docquier, Frédéric, B. Lindsay Lowell and Abdeslam Marfouk, *A Gendered Assessment of Highly Skilled Emigration* (2009).

Dunn, Andrew, 'The "Dole or Drudgery" Dilemma', *Social Policy & Administration*, 1, vol. 44 (2010).

Eastaway, Rob, 'Why Parents Can't Do Maths Today' (2010), http://www.bbc.co.uk/news/magazine-11258175

Engineering UK, *Engineering UK 2012: The State of Engineering,* http://www.engineeringuk.com/what_we_do/education_&_skills/engineering_uk_12.cfm

Fairlee, Robert, and Aaron Chatterji, *High Technology Entrepreneurship in Silicon Valley* (2011).

Ferguson, Niall, *The Cash Nexus: Money and Power in the Modern World, 1700–2000* (Penguin, 2001).

Ferguson, Niall, *The Ascent of Money: A Financial History of the World* (2008).

Ferguson, Niall, *Civilization* (2011).

Friedman, T., and M. Mandlebaum, *That Used to Be Us: How America Fell Behind in the World it Invented and How we can Come Back* (Little, Brown, 2011).

Hanushek, E.A., and L. Woessmann, 'The Role of Cognitive Skills in Economic Development', *Journal of Economic Literature*, 3, vol. 46 (2008).

Harford, Tim, *Adapt: Why Success Always Starts with Failure* (2011).

Harris Interactive, 'Microsoft, STEM Perceptions: Student & Parent Study – Parents and Students Weigh in on How to Inspire the Next Generation of Doctors, Scientists, Software Developers and Engineers' (2011), http://www.microsoft.com/en-us/news/presskits/citizenship/docs/STEMPerceptionsReport.pdf

Henderson, David R., *Canada's Budget Triumph* (Mercatus Center, George Mason University, 2010).

Heritage Foundation, *Index of Economic Freedom* (2011).

HM Treasury, *Reforming Britain's Economic and Financial Policy: Towards Greater Economic Stability* (Palgrave, 2002).

Hobsbawm, Eric, *Nations and Nationalism since 1780* (1990).

Hodgen, Jeremy, David Pepper, Linda Sturman and Graham Ruddock, *Is the UK an Outlier?* (Nuffield Foundation, 2010).

Isenberg, Daniel, 'Entrepreneurs and the Cult of Failure', *Harvard Business Review* (2011).

Jackson, Tim, *Prosperity without Growth: Economics for a Finite Planet* (2009).

Jamison, E.A., D.T. Jamison and E.A. Hanushek, 'The Effects of Education Quality on Income Growth and Mortality Decline', *Economics of Education Review*, 6, vol. 26 (2007).

Keegan, William, *The Prudence of Mr Brown* (Wiley, 2003).

Kellner, Peter, 'What Britishness Means to the British', in A. Gamble and T. Wright, eds, *Britishness: Perspectives on the Britishness Question* (2009).

Kounine, Laura, John Marks and Elizabeth Truss, *The Value of Mathematics* (Reform, 2008).

Krugman, Paul, *The Myth of Asia's Miracle* (1994).

Kumar, Manmohan S., and Jaejoon Woo, *Public Debt and Growth* (IMF Working Paper, 2010).

Lansbury, R.D., N. Wailes and A. Kirsh, *Globalization, Continuity and Change: The Automotive Assembly Industry* (2008).

Lee, S., D. McCann and J. Messenger, *Working Time Around the World* (Routledge, 2007).

Lehrer, Jonah, *Imagine: How Creativity Works* (2012).

Lewis, Timothy, 'Anyone for Deficits? A Short History of the D-Word in Canada's Development', *Literary Review of Canada* (2009).

Lewis, Timothy, *In the Long Run We're All Dead: The Canadian Turn to Fiscal Restraint* (UBC Press, 2003).

Lilico, Andrew, Ed Holmes and Hiba Sameen, *Controlling Spending and Government Deficits* (Policy Exchange, 2009).

Macaulay, Thomas, *History of England from the Accession of James II* (1848).

Marshall, A., *Industry and Trade* (1919).

Matthews, Derek, *The Strange Death of History Teaching* (2009).

McCollum, David, and Allan Findlay, *Trends in A8 Migration to the UK During the Recession* (ONS, 2011).

McKinsey Global Institute, *Debt and Deleveraging: Uneven Progress on the Path to Growth* (2012).

Michau, Jean-Baptiste, *European Unemployment: How Significant was a Declining Work Ethic* (CentrePiece, 2009).

nef, *21 Hours* (2010).

Nelson, Edward, and Kalin Nikolov, *UK Inflation in the 1970s and 1980s: The Role of Output Gap Mismeasurement* (Bank of England, 2001).

Neuwirth, Robert, *Stealth of Nations: The Global Rise of the Informal Economy* (Pantheon Books, 2011).

OECD, *A Family Affair: Intergenerational Social Mobility Across OECD Countries* (2010).

OECD, *Society at a Glance* (2011).

Office for Budget Responsibility, *Economic and Fiscal Outlook*, March 2012.

ONS, *International Comparisons of Productivity – 2010 – Final Estimates* (2012).

Orwell, George, *The Lion and the Unicorn* (1941).

Panel on Fair Access to the Professions, *Unleashing Aspiration* (2009).

Peston, Robert, *Brown's Britain* (Short Books, 2006).

Phelps, M., *Total Public Service Output and Productivity* (UK Centre for the Measurement of Government Activity, Office for National Statistics, 2009).

Pinker, Steven, *The Better Angels of Our Nature* (2011).

Prescott, Edward, and W.P. Carey, 'Why do Americans Work so much More than Europeans?', *Federal Reserve Bank of Minneapolis Quarterly Review* (2004).

Pritchett, L., 'Does Learning to Add Up Add Up? The Returns to Schooling in Aggregate Data', *Handbook of the Economics of Education* (2006).

Raab, Dominic, *Escaping the Strait Jacket* (CPS, 2011).

Reinhart, Carmen M., and Kenneth S. Rogoff, *This Time is Different: Eight Centuries of Financial Folly* (Princeton University Press, 2009).

Ridley, Matt, *The Rational Optimist* (Fourth Estate, 2010).

Romer, Christina D., 'Macroeconomic Policy in the 1960s: The Causes and Consequences of a Mistaken Revolution', Lecture, Economic History Association Annual Meeting, 2007.

Royal Society, *Knowledge, Networks and Nations: Global Scientific Colloboration in the 21st Century* (2011).

RSA, *Inside the Mind of a Cabbie* (2011).

Saini, A., *Geek Nation: How Indian Science is Taking Over the World* (Hodder and Stoughton, 2011).

Sandbrook, Dominic, *State of Emergency* (2010).

Sastry, Tom, and Bahram Bekhradnia, 'The Academic Experience of Students in English Universities', 2007, http://www.hepi.ac.uk/466-1309/The-Academic-Experience-of-Students-in-English-Universities-(2007-report).html

Skidmore, Chris, History in Schools (2011).

Sugar, Alan, *The Way I See It* (2011).

TaxPayers' Alliance, *The Non-Courses Report* (2007).

Truss, Elizabeth, *Academic Rigour and Social Mobility: How Low Income Students are being Kept Out of Top Jobs* (CentreForum, 2011).

Truss, Elizabeth, 'Why We Need Better Policies for Working Parents'. Article for the Institute of Directors, 2011.

Veldhuis, Niels, Jason Clemens and Milagros Palacios, *Budget Blueprint: How Lessons from Canada's 1995 Budget can be Applied Today* (Fraser Institute, 2011).

Willetts, David, *The Pinch: How the Baby Boomers Took Their Children's Future – And Why They Should Give it Back* (Atlantic Books, 2010).

Wind-Cowie, Max, and Thomas Gregor, *A Place for Pride* (Demos, 2011).

Wood, Sydney, 'The School History Curriculum in Scotland & Issues of National Identity', *International Journal of Historical Learning, Teaching and Research* (2003).

World Economic Forum, *Global Competitiveness Report 2011/12* (2012).

Index

Compiled by Sue Carlton

.

Printed in Great Britain
by Amazon